Two Feet of Faith

PERSPECTIVE MATTERS:
WHAT YOU DON'T SEE WHEN YOU DRIVE

David Britton Peel, J.D.

Memphis Area Christian Injury Lawyer

Endorsements and Client Reviews

Important for Anyone

"David's book contains important information not only for lawyers, but for anyone involved in a wreck. So much happens after the wreck, it is crucial that people know their options. This book lays it all out in an understandable way. Much like David, no stone is left unturned."

Amber Shaw
Gordon Shaw Law Group, TN

Extremely Hard Working

"Mr. Peel recently represented me in motorcycle accident. The case took a long time but he and his staff stuck with it in a professional manner that kept me at ease. When the case ended up in mediation, Mr. Peel not only wisely advised me and my wife during the process but he was on the phone with the insurance companies and hospital reducing the amount that we would pay from the settlement. This in no way increased the amount that we would pay to Mr. Peel but increased the amount of money we would keep. He didn't charge us an extra fee for this service which reflects his character and integrity. David became our friend through this process. I can't thank him enough."

Leonard

Highly Recommend

"He took my case at a very busy time of year, when no one else would help me."

Terry

An Absolute Pleasure to Work With

"Mr. Peel is an honest, hard-working, Godly man who exhibits a level of professionalism and care that is uncommon in his field. His responses are timely, his attention to detail is strong, and his character is admirable. Mr. Peel invested a level of personal interest and care in myself and my case. I didn't feel like just another number, or just another client. I felt like a real person and was treated with genuine concern and respect. As far as the case, the results that Mr. Peel has worked for have exceeded my expectations. Mr. Peel and his team are an absolute pleasure to work with, and are highly recommended."

Zack

An Honest Attorney

"Mr. Peel is the ONLY honest lawyer that I have ever dealt with. He is truly honest, caring and will truly work hard to represent you. All the lawyers that I dealt with cared about what they could get for themselves and not what was best for the client. So I would highly recommend Mr. Peel and you can rest assure that you have someone that will work in your best interest. A good Christian man of high moral principle! You will not be disappointed."

Anonymous 5-star review via Martindale-Hubbell reviews platform

Excellent and Highly Recommend

"Mr. Peel and his staff are very professional and caring. He was able to negotiate my medical bill amounts down which was a true blessing. He was also able to recover much more financial for my family and I than I could have imagined. I am very thankful he is using his God given talents to help individuals in their time for need."

Mark

Wise and Brilliant Attorney

"My husband and I first met David and Trish Peel in 1999, when he was leader of our Sunday School class at Bellevue Baptist Church in Cordova, Tennessee. It was a close-knit group of young married couples. At the time, I remember how some of us were facing difficult times in our lives, and he was always there, providing advice and navigating us through trying times. He was available to point us back on track and share scripture to help get us through the storms of life. Throughout the years, even after the class ended, he has kept in touch with his "flock." David was and is always willing to lend an ear, provide Biblical guidance to those having trouble seeing the light through the darkness of one of life's many storms, which have and will come. He has been a constant for us, a rock in tough times, a friend you can always lean on to carry you through or to provide just the advice you need to point you back to the Lord. He is a Godly man, someone who will speak truth and not just tell people what they want to hear to make them feel better.

I remember like it was yesterday being in a small group visiting in someone's home back in early 2000; our goal was to share the gospel with someone willing to listen. We were part of an Evangelism Explosion group from church and we visited the small apartment of a gentleman who was a heavy chain smoker. I remember being worried at the time because each breath I took while we were there, I gulped in lots of second-hand smoke. I was several months pregnant with my first child, and as we left, I expressed concern that all the smoke in the home from cigarette would cause harm to the baby boy in my womb. David said to me, 'Do you not think the Lord will protect your child?' I stopped worrying, instead prayed about it, and immediately felt a peace come over me.

David Peel is that kind of teacher—that kind of attorney—that kind of friend. Always pointing you to Christ. Always pointing you to Scripture. Always sending people back to the Lord, gently admonishing, constantly reminding us of who we are and what our purpose is here on this earth. It is not to serve ourselves but to serve the Lord.

I am also an attorney, like David. I have referred clients to David many times. He is a wise and brilliant attorney and he lives out this verse from Colossians 3:23 beautifully, 'Whatever work you do, do it with all your heart. Do it for the Lord and not for men.' Everyone should have a copy of his book. He is a blessing to all who know him, and he is incredibly generous with his time and willingness to share his God-given wisdom with others."

Michele Salazar, attorney at law
The Hayden Law Firm, TN

Online Profiles

Avvo: http://bit.ly/2kAXe62

Martindale: http://bit.ly/2kuFBlK

Super Lawyers: http://bit.ly/2kuQBjd

Yelp: http://bit.ly/2l1WiYR

Contents

Introduction.
Six Inches from Disaster

Movies show some incredible car chases. The hero hops in a high-performance sports car and screeches away, the villains in hot pursuit. After twists and turns, narrow misses and fiery crashes, the chase concludes with the hero escaping his pursuers.

Such scenes are filmed by stunt drivers on private tracks. If you want to produce a movie, do not expect permission to film on public roads! Even driving in a straight line with no shenanigans would be prohibited. You could not get approval for a movie star to drive a car on the highway, near ordinary motorists without special stunt training and protective gear.

You would be forbidden...from doing exactly what we do every single day.

Sure, the professional drivers might execute scary-looking stunts—like kicking a car up on two wheels, or jumping off a ramp, or blowing something up. But appropriate safeguards are in place. The stunt men might enter the most dangerous part of their day when they end filming and begin the drive home.

Separating them from death in a head-on collision is...six inches of yellow paint. On many roads, the only tools employed to protect these drivers are a paintbrush and a bucket. The impact of a head-on collision is like hitting a brick wall, but worse: accompanying each car is over 60 miles per hour of momentum.

Separating them from death in a head-on collision is...
six inches of yellow paint.

Future generations will look back in disbelief. They will be unable to comprehend that not so long ago, real-life intelligent adults drove 5,000-pound vehicles along narrow roads, separated from oncoming drivers by only inches of yellow paint. Look down to get your drink or grab your phone, and you wipe out an entire family before you glance back up. Future generations will consider this the Barbarian Age of driving.

Historically, many cities were built for carriage traffic. Horse-drawn carriages, not the modern horse-less carriages. We drive 300-horsepower vehicles down streets designed for trotting. Over a hundred people die every day from wrecks, many in big cities where cars intersect all the time.[1]

I think people do not understand that dotted lines in the middle of the road control cars' direction very little. We all drive cars and don't even think about it. We are much closer to death at any moment than we realize. Never would we allow two planes to fly so close together! A small Cessna doesn't fly much faster than a top sports car drives. But can you imagine flying two Cessna airplanes about eleven inches apart? The Blue Angels stunt team doesn't even fly them that close. Yet we do it every day on the ground.

The most dangerous part of an international airplane flight is driving between your home and the airport. Statistically, the flight is nowhere near as perilous as the drive—hard as that is to believe. According to NBC news, "Your chances of being involved in an aircraft accident are approximately 1 in 11 million. Your chances of being killed in an automobile accident are 1 in 5000.

---

[1] http://asirt.org/initiatives/informing-road-users/road-safety-facts/road-crash-statistics

The most dangerous part of your flight is the drive to the airport."[2]

The most dangerous part of an international airplane flight is driving between your home and the airport.

The only reason that we don't freak out about the dangers of driving every single day is because we're so used to it. If you tried to introduce the concept all at once to a safety-conscious culture, they would never accept it. Imagine a culture on an island somewhere who had never advanced further than the bicycle. You come in and say:

> "Here's what we are going to do. We will put you in 6,000-pound vehicles with top speeds of 120 miles per hour. Then you will drive up and down the road. It will be so convenient! The seats are comfortable—you might be tempted to sleep if you feel drowsy. You will eat and drink in the cars. You'll make phone calls and check your

---

[2] http://www.nbcnews.com/id/7549546/ns/travel-travel_tips/t/tips-fearful-flier/

texts. You will look at maps. You will drop stuff and try to pick it up. You will adjust the radio. You will talk to your passengers. All in all, distractions will abound. Everyone will be doing these things. Oh, and half of them will be driving in the opposite direction. But don't worry—we will separate you from them with a little 6-inch-wide stripe of yellow paint."

They would never accept the idea. But we have grown accustomed to the dangers, and thus we accept them without thinking.

It's like Tylenol. The main ingredient in Tylenol—acetaminophen—has been linked to liver failure. At least one paper has argued that Tylenol would not be approved by the FDA if it were submitted today as a brand-new medication.[3] But Tylenol is so ingrained in our culture that we never think, "Could there be a better way?" So with cars.

---

[3] Brown et al., "Would Acetaminophen be Approved by the FDA Today?" Accessed 5 October 2016 at s3.documentcloud.org/documents/793731/mcneil-history-by-students.pdf.

I think the day is coming when some communities will so value their members' lives, they will redesign their entire communities. They will convert two-way streets into one-way streets, preventing head-on collisions. They will create dedicated bike lanes—not just paint separating bikes from cars, but actual bike lanes with barriers. They will do the same for pedestrians. With this design, head-on impacts will be nearly impossible. And if you eliminate head-on impacts, most traffic deaths never occur.

Until then, we have to live with reality. This is a dangerous world. You have to account for risk, and shift some of the risk over to the insurance company. And then you need someone with expertise to get your claim paid, restoring some of your freedom. See, with a personal injury claim it's impossible to put time back in your time bank. Nor can we remove pain from the past. We cannot restore lost opportunities. All we can do is write a check. As paltry as that sounds, it is the only way to restore an amount of freedom. The person receives the financial means to reconstruct their life, to fill in the blank however they feel is best. It may not seem like much, but for some that check means the world.

And that is my role as a personal injury attorney: helping people put their lives back together after disastrous wrecks or other losses. If I can prevent your accident or loss from ever occurring through giving good advice, I will be ecstatic. But if not, I want to ensure you have good insurance. You need someone to help you understand how the insurance works, and to make sure you receive the benefits you deserve. If your case needs to be mediated or litigated, you need assistance there too.

That's my job.

And that is my role as a personal injury attorney: helping people put their lives back together after disastrous wrecks and losses.

As an example, I once represented the pastor of a large church. He had many ministerial duties, and he could never get much vacation time. At last he arranged to be gone for a full 10 days. Saving up his dollars and travel points paid off: he and his wife were going to go tour Ireland. A dream vacation.

The day arrives, and the pastor is with his family at the airport. He is standing behind his car unloading the trunk. And suddenly pain electrifies his left leg.

A large Mercedes has made impact with the pastor's knee, crushing it against his own car. The older couple inside is in shock, so much so that the driver doesn't think to move his foot from the gas pedal. The pastor's son—unable to free his father—flings himself onto the hood of the Mercedes and bangs on the windshield. The driver exits his trance, finally releases the accelerator, applies the brakes, and puts the car into reverse...allowing the pastor to fall to the ground with a crushed knee. In agony.

The pastor was about to leave for Ireland with his wife. Instead he ended up in surgery and rehab. Before the accident he had enjoyed running, but even after a year of rehab he could only run half as far as before.

In mediation, I secured for this pastor a six-figure settlement. What did he do with it?

He took his wife to Ireland.

But this time he brought the entire family!

They stayed longer, slept in nicer hotels, ate at better restaurants. To some degree, this wonderful family vacation compensated for the losses he sustained. The pastor and his wife returned from Ireland with a very nice pen as a gift for me. They told me, "You made this trip possible." That pen still sits on my personal bookshelf.

> *To some degree, this wonderful family vacation compensated for the losses he sustained. They told me, "You made this trip possible."*

The book you are now reading is a paperback extension of my legal practice. I want to educate you about personal injury cases, so that you are better equipped to make decisions in the future.

If you take these tips to heart, maybe you will never need to hire me!

How Should I Use This Book?

Almost everything you think you know about the law is wrong.

Don't take that personally—I thought I knew a lot about law too. At least before attending law school. Then came the realization that I had been severely misinformed. It wasn't that people lied to me; they were just mistaken.

> *Almost everything you think you know about the law is wrong.*

For instance: I thought that if you got hurt on someone else's property, it was always your fault. That's not true—the law is more nuanced. I believed that a driver who rear-ended another driver was automatically at fault. Neither is that true. Usually that is the case; however, it's not automatic. In reality, the law is rarely automatic. There is always an argument to be made the other way.

Remember when O.J. Simpson was found *not guilty* in his criminal trial, he was then sued civilly by the family? Many people were walking around saying, "That violates double jeopardy. It's in our U.S. Constitution." This revealed that they had been misinformed, or never looked it up for themselves. If you read the Double Jeopardy Clause of the Fifth Amendment, it states that a person shall not "be subject for the same offence to be twice put in jeopardy of life or limb." Obviously, being sued for money in no way endangers your life or limb. O.J. lost that trial, was found liable for the deaths, had a monetary judgment rendered against him, and fled to debtor's paradise in Florida to avoid payment. The second trial was not a

violation of double jeopardy.

Sometimes people are in a wreck with an underinsured driver. Even if it was not their fault, people think they should not involve their own insurance company—

because supposedly it will make their premiums increase. But according to the law in Tennessee, insurance companies cannot use such an accident against you. It is reflected as activity in your account, but no more. As I write this book, I am shopping insurance plans for my family. Each company pulls up the activity of our driving history. Sure enough, it shows a collision and UM claim as prior activity. But it does not say *liability*. And liability claims are what the company cares about.

This book aims to spread true information about personal injury claims. I have written it so that you can either read straight through, or jump around. If a particular topic interests you, feel free to turn directly there. While this book maybe a type of reference work, you may use it like any other book, reading from cover to cover! Use this book to educate yourself and I'll be pleased.

The book begins with Section I, Philosophy of Law Practice. Maybe you have big legal questions, or maybe you have a potential claim: "What must I prove to have a case?" "What's the difference between mediation and trial? Which is better?" "How can a monetary settlement provide true justice, anyway?" If any of those questions interest you, check out Section I.

Section II delves into specific cases. What if you are in a motorcycle wreck? Or medical malpractice? Or a hit-and-run accident? Details on all those and more are in Section II.

Section III is a grab bag of legal lessons I have accumulated over the years. Some even expand from the legal field into life tips.

Section IV, Wrapping Up, concludes the book with a few important notes. Do you really need a lawyer? Is suing someone morally acceptable? What action steps can you take now? Section IV answers those questions.

So use this book to equip yourself. Learn about the personal injury claims system, so you can rid yourself of misinformation you've heard over the years. Who knows—you might even be able to share your newfound knowledge with a friend someday.

Section I. Frequent Law Practice Questions

What Do I Have to Prove?

You must address four distinct elements in order to present a tort (personal injury) law claim. These elements are duty, breach of duty, causation, and injury. That is: someone must have a duty to act which is breached by act or omission, proximately or directly causing damages.

If you want to translate that into the way we all talk, it comes down to this quote: "It's how you got hurt and how hurt you got." One of the hallmarks of a good attorney is being able to understand complicated things and express them in a simple and persuasive way.

> *It's how you got hurt*
> *and how hurt you got.*

How you got hurt has to be investigated by a lawyer or a law firm with the resources for a complete investigation. And also—very importantly—with the time and personal touch to talk with you, your family, and any witnesses. In my opinion, law firms do not serve their clients well by sending a low-level "runner" to your house to sign you up. Then you hear nothing for the next two months. Until one day, a letter arrives in the mail: "Sorry, we don't want to take your case." Or even worse: "We have already settled your case. Here's your check. Bye!" You need to have a say in the matter. I'll share the alternative to this impersonal approach later in this section.

The second aspect, *how hurt you got*, requires precision and empathy. Any attorney you hire must be able to understand your medical records, translate them into everyday terminology, and discuss them with you. He must be able to show how you have been affected in mediation or court. A good lawyer is a good communicator.

Every personal injury is, at its heart, *personal*. A good lawyer must understand not only the scholarly field, but also how an injury affects you, your family, and your friends. This means that bigger firms are not always better. Consider the sort of doctor you want: practicing at a large, well-resourced hospital is definitely a plus. But ultimately, much of your experience depends on the few minutes you spend with the doctor personally. The attention, the empathy, the care—these make your visit pleasurable or painful. In a sense, law practices are the same. I've gotten job offers from large firms, but I have no interest in working for them. I want to make sure I do a good job for all my clients, one to one. If any area of life should not be one-size-fits-all, it is law practice. "In one end and out the other" is not a client satisfaction strategy. Neither the medical profession nor the legal profession is served well by generalization. Rather, they are served well by personal touch.

Every personal injury is, at its heart, personal.

How you got hurt and *how hurt you got*—majorly impactful, yet often confusing. If you ever want assistance or advice, drop me a line. Whether we end up working together or not, I'm always glad to help.

How Can a Monetary Reward Be Justice?

The point of a monetary reward is not to extort as much cash as possible from the defendant. The point is personal responsibility.

As a conservative, I very much believe in responsibility. On the claimant's side, I don't represent people who make up additional injuries just to gouge the defendant. But on the other side, the defendant needs to take responsibility for his actions. For personal injury claims, monetary settlements are the chosen means of reparation.

And that's not just true in our society. As a form of civil suit, personal injury claims trace all the way back to the Old Testament. Consider the following passages and how they touch upon both liability (how you got hurt) and damages (how hurt you got).

Liability Issues

Digging a pit but failing to cover it (Exodus 21:33–34). This creates a trap similar to a slip and fall in a modern-day department store.

Not keeping a dangerous animal penned up (Exodus 21:28–30).

> If a bull gores a man or woman to death, the bull is to be stoned to death, and its meat must not be eaten. But the owner of the bull will not be held responsible.

Note the difference in liability if the ox has a history of goring:

> If, however, the bull has had the habit of goring and the owner has been warned but has not kept it penned up and it kills a man or woman, the bull is to be stoned and its owner also is to be put to death. However, if payment is demanded, the owner may redeem his life by the payment of whatever is demanded.

This is much the same law we have now, where liability is harsher if the animal is known to be vicious.

Accidental Death vs. Murder

The civil cases I deal with results from accidents—when someone negligently runs a stop sign or crosses that center line of 6 inches of yellow paint. The Bible shows us God's heart in clarifying the difference between accidents and murder:

This is the rule concerning anyone who kills a person and flees there for safety—anyone who kills a neighbor unintentionally, without malice aforethought. For instance, a man may go into the forest with his neighbor to cut wood, and as he swings his ax to fell a tree, the head may fly off and hit his neighbor and kill him. That man may flee to one of these cities and save his life. Otherwise, the avenger of blood might pursue him in a rage, overtake him if the distance is too great, and kill him even though he is not deserving of death, since he did it to his neighbor without malice aforethought. (Deuteronomy 19:4–6)

An axe head improperly attached would be **negligent**, not planned or intentional. Other biblical examples of negligence allowing your fire to get out of control and harm a neighbor's property (Exodus 22:6), as well as building a dangerous structure without a proper railing (Deuteronomy 22:8).

Damages in the Bible

Medical Care (Exodus 21:19). "He who struck [the victim] … shall have him thoroughly healed" (ESV).

Pain and Suffering (Exodus 21:22). "If people are fighting and hit a pregnant woman and she gives birth prematurely but there is no serious injury, the offender must be fined whatever the woman's husband demands and the court allows." Or as the KJV phrases it, "he shall pay as the judges determine."

"...he who struck him [the victim] ... shall provide for him to be thoroughly healed." Exodus 21:19

Loss of Earnings (Exodus 21:19). "The guilty party must pay the injured person for any loss of time."

Some view a check as base or crass. They say, "Money can't fix things" or "Money won't bring a family member back." But does any other good option exist? I have told juries, "If you can put time back into my client's time bank, do so. If you can travel back in time and prevent this from ever occurring, please don't write us a check. If you can remove my client's pain—both past and future—do that instead. But if you don't have a magic wand, here is the best solution I have to offer: give them enough money that you can walk out of here and say, 'That was a just result.' One penny too little is not just. One would be hard pressed to say that one penny too *much* is unjust—but one penny too little is certainly not true justice."

"If you can remove my client's pain—both past and future—do that instead. But if you don't have a magic wand, a check is the best solution I have to offer."

My clients are overcomers, trudging back after a difficult setback. They don't ask for anything over what is just and due. After their award, some of my clients pay their house

off, which enables them to live comfortably, even with their smaller earning potential. Some of my clients give to their struggling children; or buy a new dog; or put up a memorial to their lost loved one; or endow a scholarship to help needy students; or simply take a long vacation. The use of the award after the case is just as personal as the injury before the case.

How Important Is Integrity to My Case?

You need to have a lawyer who prizes integrity. A dishonest attorney may be able to win your case—but who's to say he will not cheat you too? One measure of integrity is what others think of your lawyer. People who know him should say, "If you need a lawyer, he's your man. He's a fine attorney. I've known him for years."

Some of the best compliments I have ever received are from mediators or lawyers I've tried cases against or settled cases with. They tell me, "When I have to pay you, you're an easy guy to pay." Sometimes they refer cases to me or hire me to handle their own cases. (Even lawyers sometimes need a lawyer.)

"When I have to pay you, you're an easy guy to pay."

Abraham Lincoln the lawyer directly addresses this issue of integrity:

"There is a vague popular belief that lawyers are necessarily dishonest. I say vague, because when we consider to what extent confidence and honors are reposed in and conferred upon lawyers by the people, it appears improbable that their impression of dishonesty is very distinct and vivid.

Yet the impression is common, almost universal. Let no young man choosing the law for a calling for a moment yield to the popular belief---resolve to be honest at all events; and if in your own judgment you cannot be an honest lawyer, resolve to be honest without being a lawyer.

Choose some other occupation, rather than one in the choosing of which you do, in advance, consent to be a knave."[4]

Client referrals are my bread and butter: the vast majority of my cases are referrals from previous clients. Recently I spoke with a lady whose case I am handling; she told me two of her friends had worked with me before, and

---

[4] Collected Works of Abraham Lincoln. Volume 2. Lincoln, Abraham, 1809-1865.

both told her: "You hired the right lawyer." That was very encouraging.

Why Is Your Law Office Small?

My law offices are not in a high-rise building. I don't occupy the penthouse suite. Why not?

Growing up, I worked my way through high school. This was not because I wouldn't have had anything to eat or wear otherwise; it was because my family valued working hard. I did all manner of jobs: Worked in shipping and receiving. Stocked shelves at Lowe's. Mopped a grocery store's floor. Sold advertising. Helped fix cars and trucks. Painted and hung signs all over town. Washed dishes in Huddle House. During some summers I worked three jobs at once.

Because of all these jobs, I have experience interacting with people from every walk of life. I look at people for who they are, not for their position or appearance.

My father taught me this too. I'm not proud of this story, but one time I messed up. I made a comment about someone wearing not very nice clothes. My father looked at me closely and said, "Let me tell you this right now. You never judge a person based on what they have. Growing up, I sometimes had only one set of clothes. I washed it over and over. It was never nice, and it was never new—but it was always clean."

My granddaddy Chaffee Peel told me stories I'll never forget about growing up as a sharecropper. My mom's dad Otis Griffin told me about growing up in rural Mississippi. His father died when he was 11 and he became the man of the house. He explained to me about what it meant to him when he made one dollar a day. Talking with people like them has taught me the value of humanity. I strive never to forget that every single person is knit together by God.

I strive never to forget that every single
person is knit together by God.

We are all much more alike than different.

I have surprised several people with my response to questions about whether I agree with so-called "interracial" marriage. I explain to them that there are only two created races in my Bible: angels and humans. And no, they should not intermarry! But Noah had three sons: Ham, Shem, and Japheth. My friends who would be called African-American or black descend mostly from Ham. My friends of Jewish heritage descend from Shem. Interestingly, Hebrews pronounce that word as "Sem," and even now we refer to those who hate Jews as "anti-Semitic." My family traces back mostly to Japheth. Note

that they were all brothers. They and their wives likely looked rather different from another, but in the end, they were brothers—and so are we. In my mind, there is only one race here on earth: the human race. We should treat each other in light of that fact.

My father was the first in my line to go to college, and he worked his way to becoming—I believe—the youngest to ever earn a Ph.D. at the then-Memphis State University. My parents provided a very comfortable upbringing and really valued education. Not everyone had my advantages. Sometimes adults come into my office who cannot read and write—by the second time they say they "forgot their glasses," I can typically figure it out. Other times I speak with FedEx pilots or neurosurgeons. No matter who they are, we can talk as two human beings and enjoy the time.

I never try to talk over people's heads. Because when other people try to talk over me, I don't appreciate it. Some information is just plain complicated, but you don't have to present it that way. Instead of telling a person they have "advanced systematic septicemia," you can call it "blood poisoning." If their car accident resulted in an "anteriorly displaced humerus," tell them their shoulder was dislocated.

That is why my office is on the ground floor: approachability. We keep it small and relatable. We let our results impress others, not our office location. You pull up to my building and walk right it—everything is handicap-accessible too. I don't need an office on the top story of some big building, because I want to relate to everyone.

And that includes my staff. I don't make them work Saturdays, even if I do occasionally. On Wednesdays, we close at 4:30 instead of 5:00, because everyone is involved in church. Driving home, changing, and eating before church is easier with that extra half hour.

We keep it small and relatable. We let our results impress others, not our office location. You can be a rocket scientist or a bricklayer. Either way, you are still a significant human being. Everyone should treat you respectfully, and I want you to always feel that I am approachable.

Why Do You Only Handle Personal Injury Cases?

In a word: focus. There are many different-sized firms with different practice areas. But even small firms can vary widely in their focus.

Smaller law firms are often forced to be general in nature. Nothing against them—that is their reality. So those attorneys gain a level of expertise in many different practice areas. Your average small-town lawyer handles divorce, bankruptcy, criminal, injury, collections, and the occasional nasty letter. They run what we call a "door practice": they take any case that walks in the door. If you are a small practitioner who needs today's retainer to pay for last week's work, you have no other option. Such lawyers will certainly take personal injury claims when they can. And they will handle the case as well as they know how. Of course, the level of know-how varies tremendously. Will they know and have the respect of the experienced insurance defense trial attorneys? Will they understand the interplay between the health insurance lien and causation and how it can affect subrogation?

> *They run what we call a "door practice": they take any case that walks in the door. If you are a small practitioner who needs today's retainer to pay for last week's work, you have no other option.*

A real estate lawyer can advise you on closings and title defects. But he might not need to be your first choice for a truck accident, just because he used to be really good friends with your Dad's golfing buddy.

The lawyer at church may set up non-profits and corporations, do some probate work, and be very nice. But might not be up-to-date on developments in modified comparative negligence in Tennessee.

That bankruptcy lawyer who helped you with your daughter's big medical bills, and then got your cousin out of a DUI, and also did crazy Aunt Harriet's fourth divorce? You know what I am going to say.

My practice is very different. The vast majority of my work focuses on a few key practice areas. And over ninety-nine percent of my annual income is contingent in nature—meaning that I never get paid a cent unless I'm successful for my clients. Only after they receive a check am I compensated for the time, effort, and knowledge poured into their case. My clients never receive a bill the whole time I am handling the case. I advance all expenses along the way as well.

For most personal injury and medical malpractice cases, the fee is one-third. Worker's comp and Social Security disability cases typically run at twenty and twenty-five percent, respectively. But again, those fees occur only when the case successfully resolves.

So I have had both the *incentive* and the *frequency* to become accomplished in my practice areas. Martindale-Hubbell is a company that rates lawyers. They send out questionnaires to other lawyers and judges to rate their colleagues. For many years, I have enjoyed the highest possible rating: AV Preeminent. One does not become recognized as Preeminent in a chosen field unless one actually has a chosen field. Focus is vital.

One does not become recognized as Preeminent in a chosen field unless one actually has a chosen field.

Nor do I work for a gigantic law firm. Big firms have to get volume results, but I have no quotas to meet. I have no billable hours to keep up with. Treating big clients preferentially so they'll stay in-house? Nope. I'm not beholden to anyone. I don't work for an insurance company—never have and never will.

> *I don't work for an insurance company—never have and never will.*

There is an alternative to the large, impersonal settlement that I mentioned in the first chapter of this section. Focused, personal care is the solution. Only an individual perspective is close enough to notice nuances, perceive variations, and secure the best possible settlement.

While my practice is certainly not enormous, it is large enough that I don't take every case. The arrangement must be mutually agreeable, to both me and you. And this is not a "rotating attorneys" practice: if I begin your case I will finish it. Sure, other attorneys work as my partners on certain cases—like complex product liability cases— but I'm always your point of contact. My finger is on your case's pulse.

People at my law practice aren't file numbers. Every case is listed by name, not file number. I know you. My office staff knows you. We focus so that we can serve you.

People at my law practice aren't file numbers. Every case is listed by name, not file number. I know you.

How Does Wisdom Affect Settling or Going to Trial?

Wisdom is essential in deciding whether to mediate or go to court. That is part of a lawyer's job, to dispense wisdom—otherwise known as advice or counsel. Abraham Lincoln once said,

> Discourage litigation. Persuade your neighbors to compromise whenever you can. As a peacemaker the lawyer has superior opportunity of being a good man. There will still be business enough.[5]

Abraham Lincoln was a lawyer for years before he ran for President. He understood that there is a difference between a fair result and a greedy result. Perhaps pursuing a case all the way to trial would not be mutually beneficial. Philippians chapter 2 tells us to look out not only for our own interests, but also for the interests of others. Even to the degree that your enemy (or your opposing counsel) is involved, I believe an attorney can

---

[5] Abraham Lincoln, *Collected Works of Abraham Lincoln*, vol. 2.

act competently and fight zealously without being foolish or hotheaded. Before you decide to go to trial, consider all the factors and act wisely.

What Do You Do with Your Fee?

Insurance company lawyers never like to pay money out. But on several occasions, attorneys I argued against have told me I'm an easy guy to pay.

The reasons?

Great Clients

Seriously, there is no substitute for having a great client to represent. If I tell you that my client is a hardworking, church-going store owner who hobbled back into work the day after his surgery so he could serve his loyal customers, you already like him. They do, too. You cannot help but pull for the hard workers. Almost all my clients tend to be like that.

Longevity

Once you have tried cases against most firms in the area, they know you can do a good job. After over 20 years of practice, I have dealt with almost every defense lawyer at some point in my career.

Attitude

It is a fallacy that only combative jerks do well at law. A precious few have, and they will never be numbered among the truly great. You can be quite nice and still very effective—we like that in our leaders, so it should not surprise us we like that in our lawyers. Philippians 2 says to look out for others' interests, not only for our own. Actually, in many cases it is possible and profitable to work with the defense to help them justify granting your claim. As the late Zig Ziglar often quipped, "You can get everything in life you want if you will just help enough other people get what they want."[6]

Stewardship

I'm not going to go out and buy another Ferrari. Or a first Ferrari, for that matter. Nor do I blow what I earn on liquor, fancy jewelry, gambling in Tunica, or any number of hedonistic pursuits. My profits go first to support my family (including travel and missions) and second to give generously to others. For instance, my family and I often volunteer in an orphanage in the Amazon. Several times I have traveled to India to train pastors. And years ago, we set up a scholarship fund in my lovely bride's name to help nursing students. Insurance company lawyers may even know how I'll use

---

[6] Zig Ziglar, Secrets of Closing the Sale (1984)

the fees, and I suspect that might make it easier to pay my client and me.

> *My profits go first to support my family (including travel and missions) and second to give generously to others.*

Top and bottom: Missions trip to the Amazon

What Is the Difference Between Fairness, Justice, and Equality?

That's not fair?

> "You keep using that word. I do not think it means what you think it means."
> – Inigo Montoya, The Princess Bride

Once when consulting a client about his will, I heard him mention that he wanted to be fair to everyone. I asked him, "Is your goal fairness or equality?" He replied, "I thought those were the same thing! Aren't they?"

Most people think so. But in reality, fairness and equality are very different. Here's how I explained it to this man:

In reality, fairness and equality are very different.

"Fairness and equality—and 'justice' too—are different words with different meanings. Think of the Olympic 100-meter race. You want an *equal* start. You want a *fair* race. You want a *just* result. You don't want an equal result—in that case the gold medal podium would have to hold eight people. And then what's the point of running the race?"

A just result—not an equal result—is the most desirable outcome. This is part of what distinguishes me from others in my conservative philosophy of life: I believe in giving people a fair process. They certainly will not have an equal start in real life. Nobody does. My own children start far behind Donald Trump's children. Yet they are still in the top 10% of worldwide starting positions. Those who want an equal start for all must answer the question: What level of equality? Do we all need to descend to the lowest common denominator? How would such a plan actually work?

In mediation or trial, the goal is not equality. Two individuals can suffer the same injury with dramatically different effects on their lives. While we may be created equal, every personal injury is just that: personal. For instance, one of my fingers has a severe cut that is scarred over, preventing me from feeling anything with the tip of that finger. That doesn't affect my law practice one iota. But if I were a surgeon, it would be a real problem.

Or take stress and anxiety disorder. If I developed such a malady, there's no way I could continue my law practice. However, I might be able to work in the back room of a shop by myself, disassembling and reassembling carburetors. Again, personal injury is eminently personal.

The implication is that someone has to take time and get to know the individual. In order to come out with a result the client is happy with, the attorney must establish a relationship. Any good attorney needs to care about his clients—for otherwise, no just result can occur.

What Are the Largest Threats to Safety in Everyday Life?

What unintentional injury is most likely to take your life?

- A gun accident?
- A fall?
- A plane crash?
- A car accident?

A fatal injury occurs every 5 minutes and a disabling injury occurs every 1.6 seconds. According to the *Report on Injuries in America, 2003*, published as part of *Injury Facts*, 2004 edition, by the National Safety Council, in 2003 there were about 27 million visits to hospital emergency departments for injuries. About 20.7 million injuries resulted in temporary or permanent disability.[7]

The leading causes of unintentional injury deaths in 2003 were:

- Motor Vehicle – 44,800

---

[7] National Safety Council, *Injury Facts: 2004 Edition*

- Falls – 16,200
- Poisoning – 13,900
- Choking – 4,300
- Drowning – 2,900
- Fires, flames, and smoke – 2,600
- Suffocation – 1,200

On roads and highways, a death caused by a motor vehicle crash occurs every 12 minutes; a disabling injury occurs every 13 seconds.

Here are some fast facts about motor vehicle crashes:

- Motor vehicle crashes are the leading cause of death for people ages 6 to 33.
- Motor vehicle crashes are the leading cause of death for teenagers.
- The age groups most affected by motor vehicle crashes are 15-24 and 75+.
- There were an estimated 5,600 pedestrian deaths and 80,000 injuries in 2003.
- There is an alcohol-related traffic death every 30 minutes and a nonfatal injury every 2 minutes.
- Bicycling resulted in about 700 deaths in collisions with motor vehicles.

The most dangerous thing about flying in a jumbo jet is the drive to the airport!

Be careful out there. If you get hurt, you will be glad if you have plenty of Uninsured/Underinsured Motorists insurance, plus some sound legal advice.

Motor vehicle crashes are the leading cause of death for teenagers.

Section II. Specific Situations

Uninsured Driver: What If the Other Driver Carries No or Little Insurance?

If you have read my blog before (davidbpeel. blogspot.com), you may know that I always recommend carrying lots of Uninsured/Underinsured/Unknown Motorists (UM) auto insurance coverage. This is a combination coverage, with all three parts included under the term "UM." Let's look at each in turn.

Unknown Motorists: What Happens If I'm in a Hit-and-Run Accident?

Your Uninsured Motorists insurance is also Unknown Motorists insurance. It is the only policy that you will turn to in a hit-and-run accident.

Once I handled a case for a gentleman who was driving home from work. It had been a long day at the office, and he was ready to be home. He pulled up to a four-way stop and looked both ways. As he began to slowly pull forward, he heard an explosion. Suddenly he felt as if he was being propelled by a rocket, spinning violently through the intersection. Dazed and confused, he could barely see through the smoke once the car stopped moving. Attached to the back of his car was another vehicle that had plowed into him—crushing it all the way to the windshield. Two young individuals had exited and were standing at the back of the vehicle.

The man sat in his car for a moment, thankful that he and they seemed to be uninjured. But then a Buick backed up to the other car, trunk to trunk. The trunk popped open, and this gentleman watched in horror as the two youths transferred at least 300 articles of clothing from one trunk to the other. Each and every piece was still wrapped in plastic, with tags hanging off of them. The youths were emptying the car as fast as they could, throwing the clothes into the Buick's trunk. Then they climbed into the Buick's backseat and sped off—leaving nothing but a destroyed car sitting in the intersection.

As it turned out, that car had been stolen earlier. So the insurance company refused to cover the damage. The company is liable for damage a vehicle causes only when it is driven by the owner or with the owner's permission. In the case of a stolen car, by definition it has not been driven with permission of the insured owner.

In the case of a stolen car, by definition it has not been driven with permission of the insured owner.

So it became a hit and run. The man contacted me to see if it was possible to find out these people's identities, as they never got arrested. I assured him that was unlikely; fortunately, it didn't really matter—because he carried Uninsured Motorists insurance. At first, he didn't really understand how it worked. So I explained to him that if you have Uninsured Motorists coverage, your own insurance company will pay for the damages in the case of a hit-and-run accident. This man received a sufficient monetary reward in the end, all because he had insured himself against the risk of hit and run drivers piloting stolen vehicles.

Uninsured Motorist: What If the Guy Who Hits Me Has No Insurance?

Above, we discussed an "unknown motorist" case. But sometimes you know who the motorist is, and it still doesn't help much.

One day I received a client into my office, who told me this story. She was sitting at a stoplight when she was suddenly propelled through the air, crossing over a nearby barrier and rolling down an embankment. She came to understand that a man driving a stolen car had careened through the intersection, literally launching her off the embankment without slowing down. The man was shot by police in a neighboring town later that day. His identity was known.

This lady was disappointed to learn that the insurance company declined to cover her injuries, because the driver was unauthorized. He had stolen the car in a carjacking. She believed she was left without options.

However, because she had Uninsured Motorist coverage, we made a claim against her own insurance company. She was able to obtain over $55,000 tax-free after she paid me and her medical bills.

Because she had Uninsured Motorist coverage, we made a claim against her own insurance company.

Oddly enough, another lady who was hit by the same driver down the road came to see me too. Sadly, her case had no chance. In order to save money, she carried only liability insurance. Her car was a total loss; she had medical bills and lost wages. But there was nothing she could do. She needed money, but there was no pocket to pull it from.

That is why I always recommend you carry plenty of UM coverage.

Underinsured Motorist: What If the Other Driver Carries Not Enough Insurance?

Now that we've covered two different cases of uninsured motorists, let's turn to underinsured motorists.

Underinsured coverage is included within UM coverage, ensuring that you have enough money available to you in the event of a tragic accident. For example, say a drunk driver plows into you from behind. You suffer a broken shoulder blade and a punctured lung.

- Your medical bills: $41,000
- Your lost wages at work: $9,000

The drunk driver carries only $25,000 worth of insurance (normal in Tennessee). If you have no UM coverage, the most you can receive in this example is $25,000. Even if you have sustained $100,000 worth of injuries, $25,000 is the most you can recover.

But what if you carry $100,000 of UM? Then you can recover up to that full amount. If you can prove a claim of $100,000, then the first amount of $25,000 will come from the drunk driver's insurance. The second amount of $75,000 will come from your own insurance company. With Underinsured Motorist coverage, your insurance company becomes liable if the other driver carries too little insurance.

UM insurance is usually inexpensive, especially on older cars. Call your agent to make sure you and your family carry plenty of it. Some agents will say UM coverage is not that important...but they do not see what I see every day.

Some agents will say UM coverage is not that important...but they do not see what I see every day.

Destroyed Vehicle: What If My Car is Totaled?

Occasionally I receive a call from someone whose main concern is that their car or truck was destroyed in the accident. While my emphasis is injury cases, I can give some advice in such situations.

Understand that the insurer only owes you the fair market value of the vehicle—not what you happen to owe to pay it off!

> *The insurer only owes you the fair market value of the vehicle—not what you happen to owe to pay it off.*

Know that you are not obligated to accept the insurer's initial offer. Research the price of your car, and not just the Blue Book value—check listings too. Recently I've been seeing insurance companies give fairer vehicle offers. They probably realized that people who get cheated on their cars are mad when injury repayment time comes around.

In the case of a partially damaged (not totaled) vehicle, you can ask for diminution of value. This refers to the lesser value of your vehicle post-accident, even after repairs. For instance, if you could have sold your car for $15,000 before the accident, you may only be able to get $12,000 now. Perhaps your car has been restored to pristine condition and is running better than ever. It doesn't matter. Because it was in an accident, the value has diminished. You can claim the difference in value ($3,000 in our example) against the insurance company.

The company doesn't like this very much. And receiving your payout will not be easy. However, I have collected money for people in the past based on diminution of value arguments. The key is to have an appraisal from an expert that sets the undamaged value before the accident, which can be compared with an appraisal after the accident.

You can claim damages for almost any result of a car accident. Track your prescriptions, even if you got them over the counter. Or maybe you had to buy a cane, or some Icy Hot. Put it all in there. If you had to repair your glasses or get your teeth fixed, those are eligible for damages. Maybe your phone was destroyed and you had to buy a new one. I've made claims for people's jeans—

very nice jeans—that the emergency workers had to cut off them.

Tractor Trailer Wreck: What If a Semi Hits Me?

Fully loaded, tractor trailers often weigh in excess of 80,000 pounds. Drivers are paid based on the number of miles they track each day, providing every incentive to violate federal laws and rest requirements.

Semi-truck versus car is not a fair fight. As a matter of physics, it's virtually impossible for the small vehicle to win.

This is why we say that a truck wreck is not a car wreck.

A truck wreck is not a car wreck.

Truckers are ruled by extensive regulations issued by FMCSA, published in the Federal Register, and compiled in the U.S. Code of Federal Regulations (CFR). Trucking companies are responsible for the driver's compliance. They are held liable for his negligence and anyone who assists or insists the truck driver violate the law:

§ 390.13: Aiding or abetting violations.

No person shall aid, abet, encourage, or require a motor carrier or its employees to violate the rules of this chapter.

For example, a car driver might need to slow down in hazardous conditions. But look at the regulations a truck driver must follow:

§ 392.14: Hazardous conditions; extreme caution.

Extreme caution in the operation of a commercial motor vehicle shall be exercised when hazardous conditions, such as those caused by snow, ice, sleet, fog, mist, rain, dust, or smoke, adversely affect visibility or traction. Speed shall be reduced when such conditions exist. If conditions become sufficiently dangerous, the operation of the commercial motor vehicle shall be discontinued and shall not be resumed until the commercial motor vehicle can be safely operated. Whenever compliance with the foregoing provisions of this rule increases hazard to passengers, the commercial motor vehicle may be operated to the nearest point at which the safety of passengers is assured.[8]

In one case I handled, a trucking firm put a new driver into the cab with minimal training. He immediately started driving long distances without proper rest. As a result, he drove straight through a stoplight and t-boned my client. The client's shoulder was so badly broken the doctors were unable to reassemble it; to this day, no shirt he owns fits him well.

The trucker was paid about 50 cents per mile for the extra miles he squeezed in—miles that caused him to be so weary he couldn't spot a full-sized pickup truck in broad daylight.

---

[8] 33 FR 19732, Dec. 25, 1968, as amended at 60 FR 38747, July 28, 1995

About the only good news is that you can be well compensated for an accident involving a tractor trailer. Contact a good lawyer who has experience with such cases. He will make sure the insurance company treats you fairly.

Motorcycle Accidents: What If I Get Hit Riding a Motorcycle?

Motorcycles are dangerous.

Absurdly dangerous.

Let me illustrate: Let's say I dare a young man to put on a helmet and get in the bed of my pickup truck. I'm going to drive 70 miles per hour down the interstate as he hangs on. "Oh, and if anything goes wrong, just jump out of the truck."

He would say I was crazy! No one would consider jumping out of a vehicle moving at 70 miles per hour. Flinging yourself through the air and hoping for the best is not a survival strategy.

However, anyone who rides a motorcycle puts himself in exactly that position. A wreck, whether at high or low speeds, will likely result in the rider becoming a human projectile. Motorcycle accidents almost always result in death or very serious bodily injury. I have friends who have lost limbs, and I have clients whose loved ones lost their lives. Wearing a helmet helps—but sometimes the head is found in the helmet many feet from the body.

A common myth is that the average person on a motorcycle is reckless. While we have all seen idiots on crotch rockets kicking up wheelies down Germantown Road, they are the exception—not the rule. The average motorcyclist is older than you might guess, and has probably been riding for quite a while. Motorcyclists tend to drive more defensively because they realize how vulnerable they are to vehicular traffic.

In 1981, a comprehensive governmental study called "The Hurt Report," found that in two-thirds of accidents involving a car and motorcycle, the driver of the car is at fault. It's all about visibility and what one expects to see.

Many cars never even notice the motorcycle in traffic. I know it's a trite saying, but looking twice can save a life.

The most common motorcycle accident that I see involves right of way. A motorcyclist is driving straight through an intersection. A car in the left-hand turn lane doesn't notice it (sometimes at night due to the single headlight) and pulls out in front. The motorcycle strikes the side of the car, which outweighs it many times over. The rider is thrown underneath the car, crushed against the side of the car, or launched dozens of feet over the top of the car.

> *The most common motorcycle accident that I see involves right of way.*

After initial impact, other traffic becomes a problem. Motorcyclists may be "thrown clear," but too often the only thing they're thrown into is more traffic. Worst-case scenario, the other vehicles are traveling too quickly to make a complete stop, and run the motorcyclist over.

Defensive driving is essential for motorcycle riders. Unfortunately, they cannot drive defensively enough to account for the kind of negligence that injures them every day. Period. It's impossible. Their family then needs help to handle the injury claims…and too often to handle organ donation. Motorcycle riding is pretty rough.

One study concluded that the typical motorcycle accident allows the motorcyclist less than two seconds to complete all collision avoidance action. Motorcycle riders in these accidents showed significant collision avoidance problems. Most would over-brake and skid the rear wheel, while under-braking the front wheel—greatly reducing collision avoidance deceleration. The ability to counter-steer and swerve was essentially absent.

The likelihood of injury is extremely high in these motorcycle accidents: 98% of multiple vehicle collisions resulted in some kind of injury to the motorcycle rider; 45% resulted in more than a minor injury. Mile for mile, driving a motorcycle is 27 times more dangerous than driving a car (based on the number of deaths).[9]

---

[9] Insurance Institute for Highway Safety, "Motorcycles." Accessed 5 October 2016 at http://www.iihs.org/iihs/topics/t/motorcycles/fatalityfacts/motorcycles.

Mile for mile, driving a motorcycle is 27 times more dangerous than driving a car.

If you choose to ride a motorcycle, that is your decision. But wear proper safety gear, drive alertly, and make sure you know a good attorney.

Pedestrian Accident: What If a Car Hits Me While I'm Walking?

Pedestrians have right of way in most cases, but they always take the worst of the accident. Sometimes they are the victim of a hit and run. It is important to understand that UM insurance also applies to your household members as pedestrians—even those without a driver's license. (See the beginning of Section II above.)

A young man was walking across a road near a railroad crossing. Because the train was passing, all of the cars were stopped. As he passed between two cars, someone felt road rage and whipped out quickly to go around the stopped cars. They whipped out at the very second this young man was stepping out from between two cars. The impact threw him up in the air; when he landed, one of his legs was facing the wrong direction with a broken femur. Reassembling his leg required multiple plates and pins. Now his leg tells the weather like he is 92 years old instead of 22.

Ultimately, I was able to recover for him the full amount of the offending driver's insurance, along with all additional available funds from his own underinsured motorist policy. Additionally, my staff and I were able to reduce required payouts to health insurance, which further increased my client's in-pocket results.

Many pedestrians die from their injuries. Tragically, the young pedestrian this car hit was killed instantly.

(Photo: Tennessee Highway Patrol)

Road Design:
Hiding in Plain Sight

The road is full of safety features and interesting design elements that you drive past every single day. Here is a selection of my favorites.

Sign Posts

The sign posts on the side of the interstate are not driven down into the ground like they used to be. They are on "kick plates," also known as "breakaways." These plates are bolted down to a separate piece, with that piece embedded in the ground. If your car hits one of the sign posts, it will "kick out" and allow your car to go underneath the large sign. The sign will wilt and fall after you pass beneath it. In the old days, sign posts used to literally bisect cars—like a giant axe. This breakaway system is a welcome upgrade.

Guard Rails

Guard rails used to be simple and straight, and rather sharp at either end. Those guard rails often wound up acting as a javelin or jousting lance, piercing the car and taking various pieces of people as it went.

Highway designers eventually rounded the ends of the guard rails. Then they added wooden posts on the ends, with metal posts only in the center, so the wooden posts would break and absorb some of the energy.

Various designs today are even better. They feature a flat "impact plate" on the end of the guardrail, which is designed to serve as a barrier between the car and the actual guardrail. The impact plate is pushed along by the car, gradually crumbling the guardrail (by design) until the car fully decelerates. These are much better than the initial designs and tend to absorb a lot more energy.

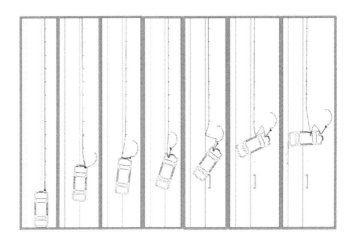

*The impact plate is pushed along by the car,
gradually crumbling the guardrail (by design)
until the car fully decelerates.*

Wire Ropes

Wire rope (or wire cable) barriers run down the center of many streets and divided highways. They are intended to prevent cross-over accidents, which are among the deadliest. Two cars traveling in opposite directions at highway speeds can do terrible damage upon collision.

Anything done to keep opposing traffic out of your lane is an advantage.

However, I believe time will show that the wire rope design is ultimately flawed in significant ways. First, it is deadly to motorcyclists, because it works to a motorcyclist's leg the way a cheese grater works to a block of cheese. Or if they slide underneath it, it works like a guillotine.

I believe time will show that the wire rope design is ultimately flawed in significant ways.

Second, while the posts holding the wire are fairly stout, I've handled at least one case where a tractor trailer broke through the posts. It entered the median, but was yanked back into a lane by the wire ropes—causing more accidents than would have occurred without them.

Finally, from a practical standpoint, police and fire and emergency responders cannot get across the interstate when they need to. They have to drive to an authorized crossing, and there are surprisingly few of those. This can actually delay responses in an emergency, and also prevents law enforcement from responding to an erratic driver. From a practical standpoint, something a little less permanent or with more gaps in it may be preferred. It occurs to me that mounded dirt berms along the median could be effective.

Fitch Barrels

In front of large bridge pilings and near highway exits, you may notice large yellow cans. Called **Fitch Barrels** (after their creator, racer John Cooper Fitch), they are filled with various amounts of sand. If you hit the plastic buckets, they will collapse and absorb your impact energy. This should prevent a blunt force injury, like that which killed Princess Diana in France. Fitch barrels are very effective, and are estimated to have saved tens of thousands of lives.[10]

Photo by Verne Equinox[11]

---

[10] John Pearley Huffman, "What Happens If You Crash Into the Pointy End of a Guardrail?" Accessed 5 October 2016 at http://blog.carand driver.com/what-happens-if-you-crash-into-the-pointy-end-of-a-guardrail/.

[11] "FitchBarrels2008.jpg" by Verne Equinox is licensed under CC BY 3.0. Accessed 5 October 2016 at https://commons.wikimedia.org/wiki/File:FitchBarrels2008.jpg.

Fog Lines

We all know about the yellow line that separates us from the opposing traffic. But we often forget about the white line on the right-hand side of the road, known as a "fog line." Often the fog line has grooves carved into it, providing a visceral sense of dismay when you stray off the road. It's a simple and cost-effective way to wake up a drowsy driver and cause them to correct course. With the current plague of texting and driving, grooving may prove just as effective at getting people to look up from their phones.

> *With the current plague of texting and driving, grooving may prove just as effective at getting people to look up from their phones.*

Some modern vehicles' safety design reflects this road feature. Lane departure warnings vibrate on the side of your seat as you move in that direction, intuitively communicating the danger.

Interstate Layout

Interstates confuse many. But if you take the time to understand how they were engineered, the layout becomes intuitive. Most people are just never taught about it.

The US interstate system features odd numbers for all interstates running north-south, starting at I-5 on the West Coast in California and going to I-95 on the East Coast. Similarly, the east-west interstates numbered evenly, from I-10 near New Orleans to I-90 near Canada.

Further, each of the spurs or loops on the interstate system is named by a particular coding system that predicts what you'll find. If the spur/loop begins with an even number—such as 240 around Memphis or 440 around Little Rock—you will find it to be a complete loop. However, if it begins in an odd number, you will find that it is merely a spur. Essentially, it is a long on-ramp that runs one direction but does not make a loop. As an example, I-155 near Dyersburg, Tennessee is a spur of I-55. It crosses the river, and that's all. It doesn't loop around to anywhere else.

Exit Numbers

A common-sense feature that many people have never been taught is that exit numbers correspond to mile markers. If you are on Exit 14 and you want to eat at a restaurant off Exit 29, you know you are 15 miles away.

The mile markers start over whenever you enter a new state.

To get more detailed, an exit sign is always on the same side of the interstate as the exit itself. Rare places feature an exit on the left, and you'll notice they move the exit sign to the left as an indicator.

White Dashed Line

We talked about the fog line and the yellow line. How about the white dashed line separating lanes that travel the same direction? How long do you think the dashes are?

How about the white dashed line separating lanes that travel the same direction? How long do you think the dashes are?

Most people answer "two feet."

But they're off by a factor of five. By law, every white dash is 10 feet long. The space in between is 30 feet long.[12] So these dashes, which in reality are as long as a basketball goal is high, are dramatically underestimated.

This tells you that your perception while driving a car is not entirely accurate, especially at a high speed. Perception on the roadway has to be accounted for in roadway design...and while driving.

---

[12] United Press International, "Many underestimate white dashed lines." Accessed 5 October 2016 at http://www.upi.com/Many-underestimate-white-dashed-lines/36181233688383/.

The Future of Highways: How Can We Improve Safety?

I'm fond of saying that we live in the Barbarian Age of driving. But we won't really know until we look back on this a few years hence.

The idea that we have traffic opposing us, with merely six inches of yellow paint separating us from a deadly head-on collision, will one day be unthinkable.

And it's not as if we have not dealt with this in some manner. We now have steel cables that provide some crossover protection. In many areas, "Jersey barriers" (those ubiquitous concrete barriers) separate the lanes. Other places, giant grass medians separate opposing traffic.

However, I am critical of the most common medians. These are often merely large grass-lined gradual ditches.

If you begin to cross over the median, there is generally nothing to stop you. In fact, gravity will pull you down towards the shallow ditch—then back up the other side with your remaining momentum. Worse yet: Even on a fairly dry day, the moisture contained in the blades of grass you are smashing at 75 MPH now coats your tires, minimizing traction in the grassy areas. Now your steering and brake input are lessened. You're a speeding hockey puck with no control whatsoever. Soon you will be launched onto the other set of lanes, into oncoming traffic. You may be struck by oncoming traffic in a sideways collision—what we call being "t-boned"—and those are rarely survived at highway speed.

Yes, the steel cables do sometimes prevent crossover. But often they do not. They may even sling somebody back onto the road in front of opposing traffic. I once had a case where a tractor-trailer's driver drifted off to sleep, crossed the median, and was headed to the trees on the opposite side—until the cables caught his vehicle enough to turn him back, straight into a head-on collision with another tractor-trailer (the one driven by my client). This Mississippi accident shows that these cables have limitations. They can sometimes cause an accident that would not have otherwise happened. Moreover, a motorcyclist hitting those cables would effectively go through a cheese grater.

At any rate, I think the medians should be inverted. They should be *ridges* or *berms* that separate the two lanes. The advantages of this are so enormous that I believe they offset any incurred costs or necessary efforts. I think this is how medians should have been designed at the very beginning.

Separating opposing lanes by a ridge or berm instead of a median is a much-improved solution that takes relatively little more room than our current medians. Berms have enormous advantages and (I would argue) very few disadvantages.

Taking this one step further, we could separate car lanes and trucks lanes with berms. If you have a set of lines for westbound trucks fully separated from a set of lanes for westbound cars, then crossover accidents become a thing of the past. Crossover head-on accidents are the most severe accidents. And the worst type of crossover accidents is when a car and a tractor-trailer collide. Can

747 vs. Cessna

you begin to comprehend the mismatch? It's like a sumo wrestler facing off against a toddler.

Do you want an 87,000-pound tractor-trailer on the same road as your 2,500-pound Hyundai? Well, do you want a 747 airplane on the same runway as your Cessna? It's worth some thought.

> *Do you want an 87,000-pound tractor trailer on the same road as your 2,500 pound Hyundai? Well, do you want a 747 airplane on the same runway as your Cessna?*

Until then, we have to live with reality. This is a dangerous world. You have to account for risk, and shift If we care enough about safety, we will have to redesign the highway system. This drawing of mine illustrates one proposal:

This new interstate-style road has earthen berms to separate the east- and westbound divided lanes. The outer two sets of lowered lanes are for tractor-trailers only. The inner two sets host automobile traffic and motorcycles.

What are the advantages of this system? There are many:

- **Block noise pollution between lanes.** No longer would you in your car have to endure the constant traffic and noise of 18-wheelers.

- **Block noise pollution from affecting the surrounding countryside.** This is a huge advantage to those bordering the interstate. They would not have to worry about out-of-control cars coming onto their property. They would no longer endure the constant traffic noise projected onto their property. Now the noise would be projected upwards and out above each berm.

- **Eliminate headlight blindness.** This is a huge problem, especially for aging baby boomers. Our eyes cannot recover from glare nearly as well as we age. We all know that some drivers can't seem to figure out the difference between high beams and low beams. As a result, you are often blinded by oncoming traffic. That has real consequences if wildlife or a stopped car happens to be in front of you. Remember: When you are going just 60 miles an hour, you travel around 88 feet per second. That is not a lot of time for your brain to perceive the danger with your eyes, send a signal to your brake foot and steering hands, and allow the car to have time to respond. It literally comes down to milliseconds between an accident and a near-miss.

- **No motorcyclists on truck lanes.** Think about the motorcyclist riding behind a tractor-trailer that loses a retread (a tire casing for worn tires). His bike may crash or flip if he hits that gigantic piece of rubber. The retread may lay on the highway for some time, and be thrown around by more tractor trailers for hours.

- **Contain "hazmat" spills.** Since tractor-trailers often carry hazardous materials like gasoline and Bromine, tractor-trailer accidents involve a whole new level of danger. Enclosed within a berm on each side, hazmat spills would never spread into oncoming lanes or affect nearby populations.

- **Contain fires.** Similarly, in the case of an explosion from a tractor-trailer gas truck, its force would be directed upward—not sideways toward oncoming lanes or nearby neighbors.

- **Eliminate crossover accidents.** This is by far the most exciting and world-changing effect of this idea. Crossover accidents are the deadliest we experience, but are also preventable by simply installing berms.

- **Safer exits.** Exits would be safer because car exits would be for car-friendly routes, whereas truck exits would be routed only to truck routes.

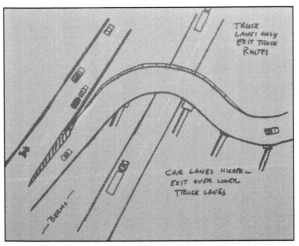

- **No sitting behind two tractor-trailers forever!** Not a single car wants to sit behind two tractor-trailers running slowly, apparently talking to one another while blocking both lanes of traffic. In addition, the tractor-trailers would rather not have cars—which they refer to as "four wheelers"—surrounding them.

- **Evacuation route.** You can easily reverse direction on any of the lanes to increase traffic flow away from a natural disaster or terrorist threat.

- **Prevent rubbernecking.** If you can't see the accident in the next lane over, you won't look at it. This is safer and keeps traffic moving more efficiently.

- **Safer police stops.** When the police have a car pulled over, the entire interstate often comes to a near stop. This is because police lights are disorienting and shine in all directions. With berms, something happening in the lanes on the other side wouldn't affect you in the slightest. Again, this maintains speed, and also prevents rubbernecking and rear-end collisions.

- **Beautification and natural habitat.** As we all know, the honeybees are struggling with the loss of their habitat and lack of wild intermixed plantings. These berms could host trees, bushes, and wildflowers strewn about as each community wishes. I imagine bluebonnets gracing berms throughout Texas, and buttercups greeting the spring near me.

- **Cost of maintenance**. If the berms are allowed to grow wild without mowing, that would save money. And unlike crashes into cables, crashes into dirt rarely require "dirt repairs."

What are the disadvantages?

- **Cost to build.** Obviously, this infrastructure update would cost more than sticking with the status quo. The width of some right-of-ways may well accommodate this update without further land purchasing.

- **Crossing over.** You would only be able to cross over and change direction at designated spots. U-turns would be rare. However, that is true with the current cable barriers.

- **Exit restrictions.** These may be inconvenient at times.

- **No billboards.** Well, this is a disadvantage for the billboard companies. Personally, I'd like it.

Some metropolitan areas already have truck highways separate from auto highways: I-5 and SR-14 in the Los

Angeles area are two examples. The state of Georgia is planning to spend $2 billion to build a 38-mile-long truck highway along I-75.[13] Extending this concept to other highways with substantial tractor-trailer traffic would reduce traffic accidents and fatalities.

---

[13] https://www.trucks.com/2016/05/02/georgia-plans-truck-only-roadway-to-fight-traffic/

Car Safety:
Are Vehicles Today Safer?

Not only roadways but also cars have become safer. Nowadays, vehicles have all kinds of wonderful features that formerly were absent. In the 1950s, steering columns would often be bolted to the car's front axle. And their steering wheel horn mechanism was shaped like a spiked blade. In many accidents that could have been survived, the front axle rammed the steering wheel into the driver's chest—like the iron shaft of Neptune's spear. Decades ago that fatal injury was common. You may not realize it, but your steering column now has multiple break points that will prevent that from happening.

I could go on to mention airbags, seat belts, collision detection devices, collision avoidance devices, automatic braking, lane departure warnings, and many other beautiful things I have written about in my online articles. Your fuel pump shuts off in the event of a crash. Some cars call 911 for you. Even the simple addition of rear-seat shoulder belts (as opposed to only lap belts) has made a huge difference. Lap belts contributed to paralysis as a result of wrecks, and were easier to be thrown from.

Following a crash, many people are terrified because they see a lot of smoke in the car. However, it is typically just powder and smoke from the airbags. A car bursting into flames is very unusual. It does happen, but is unlikely. If you see smoke and don't smell anything burning, it's probably just the airbag residue.

Here's one last cool feature you use every time you drive, but probably never think about. Your car windshield is not regular glass. It's *laminated automotive glass*, which doesn't break like regular glass and is many times stronger. Here's what a HowStuffWorks article says about this remarkable glass:

> The strength of laminated automotive glass allows it to perform two very important functions in cars. **First, it allows the passenger-side air bag to deploy correctly.** Driver's side air bags tend to fly straight toward the driver from the steering wheel, but when the passenger air bag is deployed, it bounces off the windshield toward the passenger. An air bag deploys with incredible speed -- 1/30th of a second -- and can withstand 2,000 pounds (907 kilograms) of force. The windshield has to absorb both the speed and force of the air bag in order to protect the passenger in an accident.

Because of its strength, laminated glass can keep occupants inside the car during an accident. In the past, occupants could be ejected through the windshield because the glass wasn't strong enough, but today's windshields provide more security.

In addition to absorbing the force of deployed air bags and keeping passengers inside the vehicle, **laminated windshields also provide strength to a car's roof**. Windshields keep the roof from buckling and crashing down on passengers completely during a rollover. Without the rigidity and strength of laminated glass windshields, many roofs would pose greater risks to passengers in certain kinds of accidents.[14]

As a result of all these car safety features, traffic deaths are markedly down. They are down even with drunk drivers, texting and driving, and much more powerful cars. Actually, the average unmodified minivan today could beat many of the muscle cars of the fifties and

---

[14] Christopher Neiger, "How Automotive Glass Works." Accessed 5 October 2016 at http://auto.howstuffworks.com/car-driving-safety/safety-regulatory-devices/auto-glass.htm/printable. Emphasis added.

sixties in a quarter-mile race. Yet even so, traffic deaths have decreased. These safety features deserve the credit.

As a result of all these car safety features, traffic deaths are markedly down.

Professional Negligence: What If an Expert Errs?

Various types of professional negligence have the potential to harm you. This section overviews the major kinds.

Medical Malpractice

Medical malpractice cases may be the most difficult cases in the state of Tennessee. Over 88% of reported cases are won by the doctors. The absolute clearest cases—such as cutting off the wrong leg—are settled fairly quickly. Everything else is in a gray area. This is because Tennessee requires claimants to prove that the doctor had a duty to follow a standard of care, and that his deviation from that standard of care was so unreasonable in that community as to be negligent. This allows for a broad range of interpretations and judgment calls—and even poor results. The commission or omission has to be found to be below the acceptable minimal standard of care.

> *The absolute clearest cases—such as cutting off*
> *the wrong leg—are settled fairly quickly.*
> *Everything else is in a gray area.*

Most of the time, people who call me with medical malpractice cases have experienced genuine malpractice. However, they often have not suffered damages directly resulting from the malpractice that would not have happened otherwise.

For example, I still recall a case that I was very excited about when I first met with the lady as a young lawyer. She had been going to her primary care physician for many months with persistent female trouble, including spotting. The primary care physician did Pap smear after Pap smear, but never recommended anything different.

After about a year and a half of this pain and cramping and spotting, she finally went to a Gynecologist. The first thing the OBGYN did was ask for the records to be faxed over. He sat and read the records with the client in the room, one page at a time as they printed off an old fax machine. As he studied the records the OBGYN asked her:

> "When did you have the cancer removed?"

She replied, "What are you talking about?"

"Well, it says right here on these lab results, one after another, that you had uterine cancer. You mean you haven't had surgery?"

"No. This is the first time I've heard of that cancer."

"Wow. The quack didn't even read his lab reports."

I thought this would be a cut-and-dried case. Unfortunately, I couldn't help the lady, and here's why. The cancer was stage 2 when it should have been caught by the primary care physician after the Pap smears. After the OBGYN noticed it and they performed surgery, the cancer was still at stage 2. In effect, this lady underwent the same exact surgery she would have had anyway, and the delay made no significant difference.

Therefore, she did not sustain damages that would not have happened otherwise. At best, you could claim damages for continued months of cramping. However, with the average $50,000 out-of-pocket cost to prosecute such a case, it wasn't worth it. Even though it was obvious malpractice, I couldn't take the case.

One successful medical malpractice case I was involved in related to a hospital mishandling a birth, resulting in permanent problems. Another had a nursing home not taking care of wounds, so that they became chronically infected bedsores that led to sepsis and killed the patient.

Despite such successes, all medical malpractice cases are very hard and very expensive. The case is stacked against you. That was before tort reform damage caps were instituted on the amount you can receive in Tennessee, which makes things even worse.

One of the factors complicating medical malpractice cases is the idea of *accepted risks*. Many problems that occur with hospital care and doctor's care are within the range of "reasonable care." Here's a quick list of problems due to medical care that are not necessarily malpractice:

- During the implantation of a pacemaker, a lung may be punctured, creating a pneumothorax (collapsed lung).
- During a hysterectomy, bladder punctures can and do occur, causing many related problems.
- During a spinal block with anesthesia, nerve damage (usually transient in nature) often occurs because the procedure is blind. Doctors cannot

see where the needle is going—they are forced to feel for it, and can inadvertently hit the spinal nerves.

Accepted risks of procedures are not necessarily malpractice, nor are bad outcomes necessarily malpractice. Some surgical outcomes are terrible, even though everything is done in accordance with the standard of care. A successful medical malpractice case must establish a violation of the standard of care—which means you've breached even the most minimal standard of care in that community.

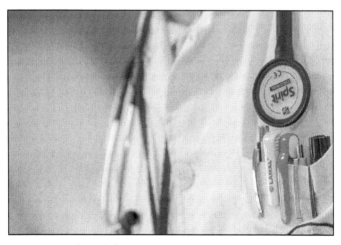

Moreover, the violation must directly and proximately cause an injury that would not have otherwise occurred.

In that aspect, medical malpractice is very different from criminal law. Watching some crazy criminal law show on TV, you may hear of a man who jumped out of a building and was falling 100 stories to his certain death. But then someone shot him as he fell, killing him prior to his impact with the ground. This wacky example would still result in a first-degree murder charge.

However, in a medical malpractice case, say you are already "falling to the ground" and the malpractice causes your death to occur a few moments sooner. I would argue that no lawyer worth his salt would take the case, because malpractice claims require you to show an impact that would not otherwise have occurred.

Recall the example I gave earlier about the girl with the Pap smears and uterine cancer. She ultimately had the exact same surgery she would have had otherwise. No acceptable risk was present, and not reading the lab reports was definitely a violation of standard care. However, at the end of the day, she was in effect no worse off than she would have been otherwise. That makes medical malpractice cases difficult in Tennessee, which is why doctors tend to win 88% of the trials and about 95% of the rural cases.

Pharmacy Malpractice

Pharmacy malpractice is a related issue. My office routinely receives calls about the wrong medication being given by a pharmacy. Given the volume that most pharmacies distribute, some mistakes are understandable. That said, most pharmacies are set up to at least have a double-check system, to avoid the wrong pill being dispensed in the right bottle. They also guard against contraindications, where one drug is already being given, and the next prescription would adversely affect the patient if the two were taken together.

Thankfully, most pharmacy malpractice cases are headed off by patients themselves. They realize their pill looks different than normal, or they notice the wrong person's name on their medicine bottle.

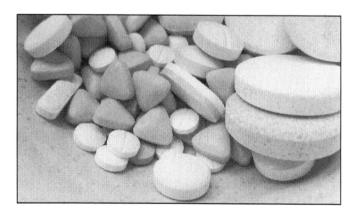

People like me who are regularly exposed to pharmacy malpractice cases take additional steps to secure themselves and their family. They routinely look up any unfamiliar new prescriptions, to make sure they know what the pills look like. This information is freely available on the web. I recommend this as a safeguard for you and your family, even to make sure that your family's medications are not swapped into the wrong bottle. Such accidents happen more than you might guess, but they are usually caught before serious damage occurs.

> *Such accidents happen more than you might guess, but they are usually caught before serious damage occurs.*

Fortunately, the pharmacological half-life of most drugs is rather short. They are not so potent as to cause long-term damage to most people. Actually, the drug companies wish they had more effective drugs—but they don't. Most drugs are out of your system in 12 hours.

Recently, I handled a case where a local pharmacy swapped the mother's pills with her child's. The child went without his asthma medication, instead receiving his mother's muscle relaxers. Even though he was in a drug-induced stupor, he was forced to go to school by his mother—who didn't understand that he had been given the wrong medicine. She was taking his asthma medication, wondering why she was in pain with an upset stomach. Well, because she wasn't getting her muscle relaxers and was taking a whole lot of asthma medication she didn't need!

The child thankfully did not suffer an asthma attack during this time—that would have changed the case quite a bit. But a pharmacy malpractice case with light impact usually resolves for a very modest sum.

Dental Malpractice

Dental malpractice is not a type of case I usually take. Once I did handle a dental malpractice case where a local dentist inexplicably pulled two permanent teeth in a child's mouth. Unfortunately, they were the two biggest teeth that everything anchored to. So the child was going to have to undergo the painful process of multiple implants in order to maintain her jaw system's integrity. I did handle that case and secured a recovery; however, I don't usually accept dental malpractice cases.

Legal Malpractice

Legal malpractice is a final category. This can happen in various ways, but by far the most common form is missing the statute of limitations. In Tennessee, a lawyer like me generally has one year from the date of the action to file a lawsuit. Every so often well-meaning lawyers miss the one-year date. In that case, the lawyer's own errors and omissions insurance must pay the claim of the injured party. It's a little bit ironic. The injured party can use the information the lawyer provided about how good his case was, against the lawyer himself.

That's professional negligence in a nutshell.

> *The injured party can use the information the lawyer provided about how good his case was, against the lawyer himself.*

Workers' Compensation: What If I'm Injured at Work?

In the 1800s, quite a few workers were grievously injured laying the railroad tracks across the western United States. If they survived the initial injury, they often did not survive the Civil War-era medical care they were sometimes provided. Often, they would be left to leave for home with nothing. Remember, that this was a time in history when there were no Social Security benefits and there were no food stamps. Only the church provided a safety net, in the form of a poorhouse for these injured individuals.

Then, they could sue their employer in common law. However, there were three defenses that stopped their case cold, so the employee lost almost every lawsuit that was brought. These three defenses became known as the "unholy trinity." The first was "Contributory negligence" which means you have something to do with causing your own injury. The second is related, called "Assumption of the risk." If you assume the risk of an injury, you put yourself in position to be hurt. And then finally the

"Fellow servant doctrine." This states that your injury is the fault of a coworker, and you cannot recover against your company for that.

Most people are surprised to learn that workers back then were able to pursue jury trials against their employer. Depending on who you read, up to 98% of these cases failed because of the three defenses mentioned above. In a few cases, they were successful and got the equivalent of a verdict of millions of dollars.

However, the system was unpopular since most employees got no medical care, had no money coming in, often had a bad recovery and wound up broke, disabled and unemployable. While a few employees wound up with the equivalent of millions of dollars, something had to change. The United States looked to England and adopted a variation of its coal mining compensation system into what we now have as Workers' Compensation.

The good news about Workers' Compensation today is that fault is not generally considered a defense and medical care is unlimited in money that can be spent. Temporary disability benefits begin when the authorized treating physician takes an employee off work.

Temporary disability benefits are usually two-thirds of the injured worker's average weekly wages earned during the 52 weeks prior to the injury. Reimbursement for

mileage to and from medical treatment may be requested if travel exceeds 15 miles.

However, if the employers are going to give away those kinds of advantages, you know they received something in return. They get to pick the list of three doctors you choose from, and they get to place the value of your injury on a schedule that maxes out at a relatively low number. Finally, they also were able to make these cases be handled by judges rather than juries. As limited as the Workers' Compensation Act has been, in July 2014 it was gutted.

Initial Permanent Partial Disability Benefits

When an injured employee reaches maximum medical improvement, the treating physician will determine whether the employee has any permanent impairment because of the work injury. If the physician believes that the employee has a permanent impairment, the physician will evaluate the employee under the American Medical Association Guides to the Evaluation of Permanent Impairment (often called "the Guides"). The Guides set forth standards by which a physician can evaluate whether the employee should receive a permanent partial impairment rating. This number will be given as a percentage of impairment. If the Guides allow for an impairment rating for an employee's particular situation, then the employee may be entitled to permanent partial disability benefits.

Workers' compensation uses a formula to determine the amount of permanent partial disability benefits an employee may receive, based on the employee's comp rate and permanent partial impairment rating. The maximum amount an employee can receive for permanent partial disability is 450 weeks of benefits at his or her compensation rate. An employee's impairment rating helps determine what percentage of this maximum 450 weeks an employee may receive. The initial permanent partial disability award is equal to the injured employee's impairment rating, multiplied by 450 weeks, multiplied by his or her compensation rate.

Increased Permanent Partial Disability Benefits

The formula above applies to initial awards of permanent partial disability benefits. Under some circumstances, injured employees may be entitled to additional permanent partial disability benefits. Usually, an employee has to wait the number of weeks represented by the initial permanent partial disability award after maximum medical improvement to see if he or she is eligible for these increased benefits.

Calculating Initial Permanent Partial Disability Benefits

Example: After Will Worker's July 1, 2014 back injury, his doctor has decided he reached maximum medical improvement on January 1, 2015. After evaluating him according to the Guides, the doctor assigns an impairment rating of 8 percent. Given his compensation rate of $333.33, Will's initial permanent partial disability award will be calculated as follows.

If the employee has not returned to work or is earning less, his or her award is increased by multiplying it by

1.35. In addition, the award can be further increased by the product of the following factors:

- 1.45 | If the employee lacks a high school diploma or a general equivalency diploma;
- 1.2 | If the employee is over 40 years old at the end of the initial award period;
- 1.3 | If the unemployment rate in the Tennessee county where the employee was working for the employer on the date of injury was two percentage points higher than the yearly average unemployment rate in Tennessee according to the yearly average unemployment rate for the year immediately prior to the expiration of the initial award period.

After these increases, the employer is given credit for the amount paid in initial benefits against any increased award.

Most plaintiff lawyers no longer handle Worker's Compensation cases unless the injuries are clearly career-ending.

Traffic Stop: What If the Police Pull Me Over?

If you are pulled over by police, roll down the windows and put your hands on the steering wheel while waiting for instructions. (If at night, also turn on your dome light.)

This may seem artificially docile, but it assures the police officer that you are no threat to him or her. With most SUVs having tinted windows in the back, rolling down those windows is confirmation that no one is waiting to ambush him or her. And while none of us law-abiding citizens would mean any harm towards a police officer, there are people who do. In addition, be mindful that sometimes you might be pulled over because your description matches someone who just fled a scene of violent crime. And he or she doesn't know for sure whether or not the person is in your car having stolen it or whether it's you.

If you are pulled over on a highway, be mindful that the police officer may approach you from the passenger side to help lessen the chance of a traffic strike. It is one of the leading causes of death of law-enforcement agencies.

If you have any firearms in your vehicle, you're under no obligation to reveal that unless you are asked. But if you are asked to, it is prudent to simply disclose the location of the firearm and then ask the police officer how he'd like to handle things.

Years ago, it was common to exit the vehicle and approach the police officer. Now, that is generally seen as an active threat. However, if you were being stopped in suspicion of a felony, a felony stop will ask you to exit the vehicle. The general procedure is that the lights will be trying to warn you and shine lights in your mirrors to blind you. Police officers will exit their vehicle and hide behind their doors with guns drawn. And you will be asked to put your hands outside the window and then exit the vehicle.

The next step in this terrifying process would be usually interlocking your hands behind your head and walking backwards towards a police officer or, going down on your knees or even believe it or not, spread eagle on the ground.

I know this may seem like overkill, however the police officers who do a felony stop have a reason to believe that they are in danger from an armed violent suspect or they wouldn't be going to this much trouble.

And whether you were pulled over for a minor traffic infraction, or because of suspicion of something much worse, always be respectful to the police. Remember that the first job of that police officer is to make sure that you are not a threat to him or anyone else. That means that he or she must take control of the situation and make sure that you are harmless. That must happen before there's some debate about what you did or didn't do. So the quicker you get to the point where the officer feels no threat from you, the better it is for everyone involved.

So that means hands always visible, no quick movements, seek permission to do anything you're seeking to do (like get registration or insurance out of a glove box). My regular readers know that it's a good idea to put your insurance card on your driver side visor mirror so that anyone driving your car could easily produce proof of insurance without going through all kinds of boxes in the car.

Finally, I would suggest that it is difficult to win an argument with the police. You can make your point about why you believe a ticket should or should not be given, but I do not believe that there is ever a reason to be disrespectful. If he is wrong that is why we have judges.

Please feel free to share this with drivers that you care about to help keep them safe the next time they happen to be pulled over.

Section III. Action Steps

What Action Steps Should I Take Before an Accident?

Hope for the best and prepare for the worst.

That's the philosophy of this chapter. May you never have an accident, injury-causing or otherwise. But in case life has other plans, you need to get ready.

This chapter contains advice for preparing three areas of your life: your family, your home, and your car.

Family: How Important is Life Insurance?

The week after your funeral, would your family prefer your insurance agent bring a tuna casserole or a half-million-dollar check?

That's the rhetorical question that tells you how much life insurance matters. A rule of thumb is to insure yourself for ten times your annual salary.

Family: How Do I Set Up a "Poor Man's Disability Policy"?

Most disability policies—even if you have a private one—do not kick in for 60 to 90 days. That means you could be out of work for several months before any money comes in. Whether due to a car wreck, a work-related injury, or an accident at home, that is not an ideal situation. Planning to have expense money for about three months is critical.

Three months' worth of expenses is hard to save for most folks. But you can attack it a different way and make at least some progress. Gather your utility bills from the past few months and look at the various amounts you paid. Then start paying the *highest* amount each month, automatically. After a year or two, you will have built up a credit balance without noticing any tightness in your pocketbook.

What if you're suddenly injured and have no money to pay the electric bill? No problem. Your credit balance is positive, so you can pay nothing for several months and still be in the black. Sitting in a lightless house isn't your only option, because you've built up four months' worth of credit. That is what I call a "poor man's disability policy." And don't worry—if you sell the house, the utility companies will send your extra money back to you.

Paying utility bills in advance is an easy way to keep the pressure off. When you receive a bill in the mail saying "Credit Balance—Do Not Pay," that is very gratifying. This is a simple little habit that makes life easier. At the end of the day, you're still paying the same amount of utility bills, but ahead of time instead of in the moment. So you have a little bit of breathing room from the accident until your insurance kicks in.

Home: How Can I Protect My Home's Contents?

Create a video of your home's contents. Store a copy of the video offsite, whether at grandma's house or in a safe deposit box. After a fire or tornado or flood, if your homeowner's insurance questions what was lost, you can offer the video: "Watch it yourself and see."

You are going to have to fill out a Proof of Claim form for each and every item—its cost, age, and condition. I don't know about you, but I can't list every shirt I own. But if you quickly video them all, after a disaster you can sit in an extended-stay motel and watch the video: "Okay, blue polo shirt. I got that one in San Destin. It cost such-and-such amount. Next, green IZOD shirt...."

Aided by the video, you can list most of what you own. Submit your claims forms alongside the video, and you should be able to replace most of your possessions. Can you imagine trying to list everything you own, when everything you own is now a pile of ash? That would be a nightmare. Worse, it would be a nightmare on top of another nightmare—the disaster itself.

Aided by the video, you can list most of what you own.

Pause reading this book for 10 minutes and go take a smartphone video of your house. Walk around and scan each room—shouldn't take you too long. Then email the video to someone, or upload it to the cloud, or burn it to hard disc and store it somewhere safe. You can even put it on file with your insurance agent.

Home: What Should I Keep in My "Go Bag"?

A "Go Bag" is a packet of personal items you keep packed for each member of the family. Kept in a central location, the bag contains a change of clothes, toothbrush and toothpaste, and any other necessities. If they take medication, include several days' supply. Maybe they need a good hairbrush. Perhaps they get cold and like warm socks. Or they love to read and would die without some books. And then an extra pair of glasses so they can actually read those books. Whatever it is, you throw it into the Go Bag. Then add a copy of your living will and your power of attorney for healthcare. And you're done!

Now if you have chest pain in the middle of the night, your spouse can grab your two Go Bags as you head to the hospital. You both can survive at the hospital for a few days, without having to send people to your home to dig through your underwear drawer. Nor will the doctor come in to talk while the uninjured spouse has gone back home to fetch something. The average hospitalization only lasts a few days, so the Go Bag should enable you to stay at the hospital semi-comfortably.

Now if you have chest pain in the middle of the night, your spouse can grab your two Go Bags as you head to the hospital.

At one point or another, most of us have wished we had a change of clothes. I remember being at the hospital emergency room all night long once, covered in my son's blood after he had cut himself badly. But that set of clothes was all I had to wear. I would have loved to change and get my son's blood off of me—especially when I went in to see him—but I didn't have a choice. That's the sort of situation a Go Bag prevents.

Car: How Should Car Seats Be Installed?

Do you have your children buckled in safely?

Some of my friends in law enforcement surprise parents when they check the car seats at free inspection stations and find that the seats are not well installed.

Sometimes the rules and recommendations all seem to run together. I hope that this may be helpful to you when transporting your kids or grandkids.

As I understand it, Tennessee law requires the following.

- Under 1 year, 20 pounds or less: Rear Facing (in back seat if available)
- 1–3 years, more than 20 pounds: Front Facing (in back seat if available)
- 4–8 years: up to 4'8" Booster with Belt Positioning (in back seat if available)

Most police and fire fighters will help you make sure you understand how to have your little ones snugly buckled in their car seats. Avoid used car seats, as they may have been recalled or damaged.

> *Avoid used car seats, as they may have been recalled or damaged.*

Be sure to avoid the front seat for children if the air bag cannot be turned off, or does not automatically disengage based on weight. The air bag can turn a minimal impact into a fatal accident for a child.

Let's make sure Mom and Dad are buckled in, also! When you see the results of accidents that I investigate every week, it makes you more careful.

Car: Where Should I Store My Insurance Card?

Most people store their insurance card inside the glove compartment. That's good, but I think another location is superior: the visor. First, if someone in your house borrows your car, they don't have to search around to find the proof of insurance. Being clipped to the visor, it's always visible. Additionally, in an accident the visor tends be easier to access than the glove compartment.

Often the glove box is un-openable and near-unrecognizable following an accident—exactly when you need to prove your insurance the most.

An alternative is insurance smartphone apps. Insurance companies like State Farm and GEICO have your proof of insurance inside the app, so you can download to your device and always have it with you. But as with the glove box, your phone may not survive a wreck. Best to keep a physical copy of your insurance card in the visor just in case.

Car: How Can I Avoid Being "Upside Down" on My Car?

If your car is destroyed in an accident, the insurance company does not have to pay it off. They only owe you fair market value at the time of its destruction.

Since many cars are worth only 80% of the sticker price the moment they first exit the lot, owing more than a car is worth is very common. This is called being "upside down" with your car.

Since many cars are worth only 80% of the sticker price the moment they first exit the lot, owing more than a car is worth is very common.

Securing a better deal on the front end can reduce or eliminate the problem. That is still the most advisable route, because it costs the least total money all around.

However, there is another option worth discussing. This protection actually costs more, but can be a lifesaver. It is called "gap coverage." Gap coverage is an optional coverage that will pay the difference between your car's payoff and the amount you receive—such that you will not owe anything more if the car is totaled. Not all lenders offer it, but it is becoming more common.

Here's an example to make things clearer.

Purchase price of new car (Financed):	$20,000
Insurance company top offer on totaled car:	$15,500
Amount still owed the dealership:	**$4,500**

This is where gap coverage comes in.

Gap coverage benefit payment to lender	$4,500
Amount now owed the dealership:	**$0**

Gap coverage is most helpful in the first few years after a new car purchase. Overall, you will find that buying a car with a few thousand miles on it (rather than a brand-new car) is often cheaper all the way around. However, if you purchase a brand-new car right off the lot, check the price on gap coverage.

Also, please do not forget to have plenty of Uninsured/Underinsured Motorist coverage. Make sure that those you love do, too. And do not assume you have true full coverage unless you check it out yourself. Some low rate insurance companies sell you "full coverage" which does not include UM, rental cars, etc. Look at your *declarations page*. You should see "Uninsured Motorist Bodily Injury" included there. The lowest amount available is 25/50, but I recommend at least 100/300 UM. An umbrella policy is also advisable for higher net worth folks. Ask your agent.

What Action Steps Should I Take After an Accident?

Despite all the precautions you take, you may one day find yourself in an accident. This chapter provides the action steps you need to take, starting with the scene of the accident and moving through the claims process.

Follow This Immediate Checklist

The back of my business card contains a quick checklist of things to do immediately after an accident. If you commit this checklist to memory (or carry my business card around), you will be well prepared.

- Get safe
- Call 911
- Check on others
- Photograph scene before moving vehicles
- Photograph other driver's ID, tags, and witnesses' IDs (this is faster than writing)
- Seek emergency medical care

Go to the Doctor Immediately

Avoid self-diagnosis. After an accident, your adrenaline is running hard. This is the worst possible time to diagnose your injuries. Even if you feel all right, take the ambulance to the ER and get checked out. Almost inevitably, more problems will arise within a few hours or days of the accident. Whatever is tight on Day One is extremely painful by Day Three. Initial stiffness isn't uncomfortable—but the later throbbing is.

People tend to minimize their injuries. Now, I don't care to represent people who throw themselves onto the ground and cry, "Oh, ouch, I'm hurt so very badly"—faking serious injury. Those cases hold no interest for me. Plenty of other firms will take people who go to their house doctor and run up a fake bill. But I want to represent real people—people who unconsciously minimize their injuries. Listen to this sheepish statement: "Well, actually, I wasn't hurting at the scene. But wow, the following day, I couldn't hardly get out of bed. My neck was hurting—and I thought, oh man, they're going to think I'm faking." As opposed to the fakers, that statement actually has a ring of truth to it.

Because we tend to misdiagnose ourselves at the scene, it is important to seek emergency treatment. Take the ambulance and go to the emergency room. If you don't like ambulances, have a friend take you. The ER personnel will say the following words: "Take tomorrow off. Take this medicine. If you are not feeling better in three days, see your doctor." Almost verbatim, those will be their instructions.

Because we tend to misdiagnose ourselves at the scene, it is important to seek emergency treatment.

When you do go to see your primary care physician—who had maybe limited training in orthopedics years ago—he or she will look at you and say, "Well, it's probably whiplash." The doctor will give you some prescriptions, usually a muscle relaxer and a pain pill. Then you will be instructed to take another few days off; if you have not improved in two weeks, go see a specialist.

The specialist will be an orthopedic surgeon or a neurosurgeon. Because you are coming to them from a car accident, some specialists will not want to see you. I mean that. Even though a lot of big cases come from car accidents, their front desk staff is trained to turn down car accident patients. Why? Because of how insurance works.

If you have *medical payments coverage* on your car insurance , then your health insurance has the right (although not always exercised) to delay payment initially. To make them start paying, you must furnish proof that the medical payments coverage has already been spent. Then your health insurance should kick in and pay everything.

Exhausting the medical payments coverage funds is not difficult, since it is usually only $1,000-$5,000. But it does create one more step. Therefore, some specialists prefer to avoid seeing car accident patients.

Alternatively, a lot of health insurance plans will pay from the very beginning. That approach is far more advantageous for you, because your health insurance receives a deep discount on most of your care. We want to minimize your out-of-pocket payments, and ensuring that care is billed as cheaply as possible accomplishes that.

Do Not Delay Treatment

Going to the doctor properly is the one thing a lawyer cannot do. Almost everything else in a case we can help with: gathering medical records, obtaining the accident report, collecting photos, interviewing witnesses, measuring and photographing and checking and producing—but we cannot get medical care. We cannot see the right doctors and tell them your personal story. Only you can do that. So you must do it.

Too many people wait around a few weeks, thinking the pain will go away. Once they finally visit the doctor, they have already painted a big message on their back: "faker or exaggerator here." No matter the reality, the insurance company will cast the victim in a negative light.

> *Too many people wait around a few weeks, thinking the pain will go away.*

Unfortunately, people generally disbelieve that folks who are hurting will hesitate to visit a doctor. They think if the pain is really that bad, people will go to the doctor quickly. And if the pain was insufficient to make you visit the doctor immediately, why are you bothering to litigate about it?

Delay in treatment can be critically harmful to your case. Normally it happens among honest folks who don't want to make a big deal of things. They are not loaded with extra pocket money to spend on medical care. They don't understand the insurance issue. They are misinformed or declined by a doctor. None of this is their fault—but they still suffer the consequences. It happens all the time. Delays make your injuries seem like they were no big deal...at least until you met with a lawyer and got his advice. Delay in treatment is serious, and it can adversely affect your recovery, so pursue treatment immediately.

Note Previous Conditions

Pre-existing conditions are important. You must be able to differentiate between what you already had and what you have now. Sometimes the impact worsens previous conditions, or sometimes it decreases the effectiveness of your prescriptions. A medical professional's assistance is absolutely necessary in separating new injuries from worsened previous conditions.

Take Photographs

Photos of ugly bruises, bolted ankles, bloody seat belts, and exploded airbags all go a long way to tell a story. Always default to taking more pictures than you think you need. Even if it's your worst day, you look terrible, you don't get up early, and you don't want anyone to see you—still take them. In previous court cases I've submitted photographs of bruises across breasts and bellies. One poor lady was on the back of a motorcycle, and the boy she was riding with popped a wheelie—dragging her rear end and rubbing it raw. The pictures were horrific. Not a very flattering location on her body, yet nonetheless an impactful picture. As the old saying goes, "A picture is worth a thousand words." In court, probably a hundred thousand.

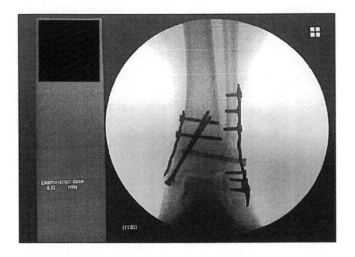

Photos of ugly bruises, bolted ankles, bloody seat belts, and exploded airbags all go a long way to tell a story.

Pictures of bad property damage are also valuable. Everyone can look at a totally destroyed vehicle and say, "Yes, I believe somebody was hurt in that." The more impactful photos you can take, the better.

Don't Talk to the Other Insurance Company

Do not talk to the other insurance company.

WARNING: DON'T GIVE STATEMENTS

Period. End of discussion. This is vital. Once I represented a man who had been driving down Germantown Road—a big divided six-lane road. As he entered the intersection under a yellow light, a car in the opposing left-hand turn lane decided to try to beat the light. It turned left directly in front of him, and a terrible collision ensued. The man was injured, though not severely. A few days later he received a call from the other driver's insurance company. He thought to himself, "The case is no issue. This should be fine." So he talked with them. He was walking through a home improvement store, with mediocre reception on his cell phone. As he shopped they kept asking him questions. When I received the transcript of the call, I realized their strategy: they asked the same question five different ways.

Do not talk to the other insurance company.

What was that question? This: "What did you do as you approached the light?" At various points in the conversation, separated by other inquiries and chatter, the company representative continually rephrased that question. On the fifth try, he finally got the response he was looking for:

> "When you saw the light turn yellow, did you brake or accelerate?"

> "I accelerated."

Once they heard him admit that he increased his speed, they could make it look like he was trying to beat the light. They denied his claim as a result of that conversation— the talk he felt was no big deal. For months after he hired me, I had to work on straightening out that discussion. It should have never occurred in the first place. Giving a statement to an insurance company is just like testifying, for most purposes. You must treat it very seriously. The company will ask a hundred questions, but a dozen different ways. They're searching for contradictions and damaging admissions.

You have probably never talked to an irate insurance professional. They always sound nice. But that demeanor is simply a means to an end. In this case, it would have been far better for my client to respond, "I am going to talk to my family attorney before I give any statements." They would have had no problem with that response. But instead he gave an extended statement, and that dropped him in hot water.

I called the insurance company to ask why they had denied my client's claim. The adjuster told me, "Because your client said he gunned it through the light."

"That's actually what he said?"

"Yep."

"Well, I'm not normally a betting person," I said, "I'll just make this a unilateral offer, so it's not gambling. You send me the audio transcript. If he actually used the phrase 'gunned it' then I will send you and your family out for a lobster dinner, on me. But if the transcript does not include that phrase, I don't want to hear any more about this denied claim. Let's move on and get it resolved." The fellow began to crawfish almost immediately on that, retreating from his position.

My client was asked whether he accelerated or braked through the light—and he said he accelerated. When you want the car to go faster you put your foot on the gas pedal. Nothing is illegal about that. Nothing is illegal about entering an intersection on a yellow light. The illegal matter is entering an intersection while the light is red. The light was yellow, so he had the right of way. Ultimately the company agreed and paid.

That case had a happy ending. But others might not. If you make a seriously damaging statement, you may jeopardize your entire claim. Never talk to the other insurance company without counsel from your attorney first.

If you make a seriously damaging statement, you may jeopardize your entire claim.

Know You Will Be Videoed

You need to realize that you are going to be videotaped. We live in a surveillance world. Sometimes traffic cameras capture the actual accident happening, which is useful in court. Other times you personally may be put under surveillance by the insurance company. If you make a substantial claim, at least one person will likely come by your house or work to video you. They will record you walking to your car, or perhaps fixing your car tire, which just lost all its air…for no apparent reason. Yes, that does happen. Especially in workers' compensation cases or serious injury claims, the company wants to videotape you engaging in activity.

Social media websites like Facebook, Twitter, and Instagram have made gathering videos much easier for insurers. Be aware that regardless of your privacy settings on social media, you must assume that the insurance adjuster and the defense attorney are watching. They are.

> *Social media websites like Facebook, Twitter, and Instagram have made gathering videos much easier for insurers.*

Once I represented a young lady who claimed she was inactive for two weeks after her injury. However, that was to the best of her memory; the accident had occurred several months earlier. But then the opposing attorney sent me a photograph he had found on one of her social media accounts: this young lady waterskiing, 11 days after her injury. He told me, "The company will only pay for treatment before this date. After the waterskiing trip, I don't buy the claim that she is still injured."

It turned out that my client had gotten the chronology mixed up in her head. It was an honest mistake, but it did limit her ability to collect. Photos and videos like that can totally destroy a claim. You need to anticipate surveillance—preferably without being paranoid. No need for foil hats. But if you are making a serious claim, especially against a large company with unlimited resources, you will be observed.

These folks can also interview your coworkers, your family, your staff, and any other people around you. One of their favorite types of people to contact is ex-wives and ex-husbands. Anyone who is mad at you becomes a potential resource for the insurer.

Hire a Lawyer You Trust

It may not be me, but hire someone you trust. Try to find someone who focuses on this area of law. You can verify if they know their stuff by checking Martindale-Hubbell.com to see how their clients and colleagues rate them. "AV Preeminent" is the highest possible rating.

Consider Mediation

Your lawyer may suggest mediation. Mediation is a process that can sometimes help parties mend matters. It is becoming quite common in the injury cases I handle. But mediation is useful in all kinds of issues. Recently, I was the mediator in a commercial real estate dispute that resolved well.

The mediator is usually an experienced attorney or retired judge, but is not actually required to be an attorney at all.

Mediation and Arbitration are two of the many forms of Alternative Dispute Resolution (ADR). In both, a neutral party is present there to help but "has no dog in the fight." In arbitration, the neutral party is called the *arbitrator* and is basically the judge. He or she decides the case after hearing all the evidence presented.

In contrast, a *mediator* does not decide anything. A mediator tries to work with both parties to find a solution that everyone can live with. There is usually not a big winner or loser; instead, each party takes control of his or her destiny. In mediation, a settlement does not occur unless *both* sides agree. In a court, the judge or jury makes all the decisions—not you.

A mediator tries to work with both parties to find a solution that everyone can live with.

Due to the delays, costs, and huge uncertainty of litigation and trial, mediation is usually worth a try. Meditation costs vary, but both sides should expect to pay between $600 and $1,000. Compared to trial, that is a pittance.

Relatedly, Proverbs 25:7-8 instructs that one should not go hastily to court: "What your eyes have seen, do not hastily bring into court, for what will you do in the end, when your neighbor puts you to shame?"[15] Within reason, settlements should be pursued.

If mediation does not reach a settlement, you can still go to trial. Anything said in mediation is not admissible in trial to be used against you.

I fully believe in the mediation process. Maybe one day I will help you mediate a dispute.

---

[15] Proverbs 25:7-8, English Standard Version.

Be Credible in Court

Credibility. While the word may be common in discussing celebrity cases like Michael Jackson's 2005 acquittal, you may not have thought much about what actually constitutes credibility.

In Jackson's case, for instance, the accuser's mother had a rather long and sordid past of lawsuits and accusations. Several of these resulted in payoffs and settlements. This apparently helped to cause a lack of credibility that some members of the jury said they perceived. And, for the record, remember that a "not guilty" verdict is NOT the same as "innocent." It means on that day in that trial, the jury was not satisfied with the state's evidence of the crime.

So, how do you define this elusive word, "credibility?" According to *Webster's Online*, credibility is:

1. the quality or power of inspiring belief;
2. or, capacity for belief.[16]

In our legal system, the "finder of fact" (the jury or judge, as the case may be) is usually the sole evaluator of

---

[16] "Credibility." Merriam-Webster Online. Accessed 5 October 2016 at http://www.merriam-webster.com/dictionary/credibility.

credibility. This is because they actually watch a witness testify in person.

I suggest that credibility is the single most important factor in the courtroom for any witness. Without it, a jury may ignore what he says altogether. In my injury, death and workers' compensation trials, my client's credibility is critical.

I suggest that credibility is the single most important factor in the courtroom for any witness.

However, a witness's credibility actually varies depending on the subject about which he is testifying. For instance, if a mechanic with 30 years of experience is called as an expert witness in a case to testify that another auto shop had installed the wrong spark plug wires on someone's car, he would likely have high credibility with a jury. He may not have high credibility with the jury about any other subject or facts.

But, on cross examination, what if it turns out that he used to work for that very shop, and he had been fired for embezzling $10,000? It may well throw his whole testimony into doubt. Why? Bias. He may be stretching the truth to get back at an enemy. He was dishonest and stole money and was caught.

Bias is a witness' own leaning or reasons for testifying a certain way. We all have biases, but most people overcome them and testify honestly. Biases not only affect what we will think, but possibly even how we perceive what we think we saw.

This is why lawyers like a *disinterested* witness. A disinterested witness is one "without a dog in the fight," so to speak. He knows no one in the case at all. He probably doesn't really care much what happens with the case. He is just there to tell what he knows or saw.

Give Accurate and Wise Testimony

Whether you are giving testimony in a deposition or in trial, realize that understanding should precede answering. Any answer you give can be used against you. Too many people cut the questioner off, beginning to answer the question before it has been fully asked. In everyday conversation we talk that way, for convenience. But in testimony you should not interrupt. You have to listen to the entire question.

Any answer you give can be used against you.

I usually ask my clients to take a breath after the question is over, to make sure that everything has processed before they begin to answer. Otherwise, you may answer *some* question accurately—but not answer the question that was actually asked. Further, people tend to give too much information. While you want to be helpful and not ugly, you also don't want to illuminate the defense lawyer as to everything you've ever done. This answer is too long:

"Do you drive an orange El Camino?"

"No. I used to have an orange car, but it wasn't an El Camino. But I got rid of it because the gas mileage was really bad, and I got this newer car. Although with this newer car, I don't know why—but I just don't really like it. I don't think I can see out of it as well."

Such chit-chat provides the opposing attorney with way too much material. Here's the right way to conduct the exchange:

"Do you drive an orange El Camino?"

"No."

Or if you want to be especially polite:

"No, I do not."

Be crisp and to the point. Listen to your counsel's advice about answering questions properly. A particular way of answering questions ensures you will be both accurate and wise.

I Have to Pay Back My Health Insurance?

Clients are always surprised to hear they are required to pay back their health insurance for medical bills covered. At first this strikes people as quite unfair. After all, they paid premiums out of every paycheck to buy this health insurance. Now they have a claim, and they have to pay the health insurance company back?

However, the fact of the matter is that their liability or uninsured motorist insurance is paying the complete claim—which includes the medical bills. Therefore, not reimbursing the company (at least a negotiated amount) means they have financed your medical bills, while you collected the cost of those bills from the liability carrier. Many would say that is double dipping.

Negotiating this process—known as "subrogation"—is sometimes even more critical than the more understood roles I play.

WARNING:

SUBROGATION AHEAD

Section IV.
Wrapping Up

Why Do I Need a Lawyer?

While you may not require a lawyer for a fender bender in a parking lot, more serious injuries have more issues then you might imagine. Realize that the insurance company and the other driver are only two of several parties that can be involved in a case.

Realize that the insurance company and the other driver are only two of several parties that can be involved in a case.

Recently, a driver was winding down a dark, two-lane, rural highway.

Headlights of a vehicle coming toward him seemed to be in the wrong place. In fact, as the two vehicles sped towards one another around a bend, the opposing truck's headlights were actually in this man's lane. They were coming right at him!

Immediately the driver took evasive action, slowing and swerving as far over as he could. However, the levee road he was traveling that fateful night offered almost no shoulder.

The sound of a ferocious impact echoed through the creek bottoms. Later, a helicopter airlifted him to the hospital with severe injuries. He is blessed to even be alive today.

The driver of the truck that caused the crash fled the scene on foot, leaving his blood all over the cab of the destroyed vehicle he was driving.

The injured client wisely carried $50,000 of Uninsured/Under-insured Motorists (UM) Coverage. However, he had sustained almost $70,000 in medical bills, as well as time lost from work. He contacted lawyers who told him they honestly felt they could do him no good. But after reading one of the articles on my website, he contacted me; upon careful investigation I accepted the case.

His health insurance had paid $32,000 for his medical bills. They were due to be paid back for that full amount. His UM policy of $50,000, with one-third of that toward the attorney's fee, would only leave $33,000 and change. After medical bills: under $1,000 remaining.

Thankfully, I was able to negotiate the health insurance payback down from $32,000 to about $10,000. This put a solid $20,000 in my client's pocket.

Can a Christian Sue According to the Bible?

As a Christian and a lawyer, I have been asked about this many times. As with any question, we should consult the Scriptures first.

The Biblical text that is most often cited is Paul's letter in 1 Corinthians 6:1-8:

> If any of you has a dispute with another, dare he take it before the ungodly for judgment instead of before the saints? Do you not know that the saints will judge the world? And if you are to judge the world, are you not competent to judge trivial cases? Do you not know that we will judge angels? How much more the things of this life! Therefore, if you have disputes about such matters, appoint as judges even men of little account in the church! I say this to shame you. Is it possible that there is nobody among you wise enough to judge a dispute between believers? But instead, one brother goes to law against another-and this in front of unbelievers! The very fact that

you have lawsuits among you means you have been completely defeated already. Why not rather be wronged? Why not rather be cheated? Instead, you yourselves cheat and do wrong, and you do this to your brothers.[17]

Let's look at the passage carefully. The kind of case in question is described in the text: a **dispute** that is **trivial** in nature **between believers**, involving being **cheated** and **wronged**. This dispute could well be judged by a **man of little account in the church**.

*The kind of case in question is described in the text: a **dispute** that is **trivial** in nature **between believers**, involving being **cheated** and **wronged**.*

Details of the actual dispute are not revealed, but from the description above it is clear that it involves a matter that is between two believers, where one feels cheated or wronged. Furthermore, the matter appears—to others at

---

[17] 1 Corinthians 6:1–8, New International Version.

least—as **trivial** in nature. The Bible expressly states that legal action in that situation is shameful.

An example of that might include a Christian church member suing another member for slander, because that member unknowingly shared partially false information in a prayer request about her—allegedly hurting her reputation. Or it could involve two members of a church suing one another over the giving of a poor reference for a job. (Yes, both of these are unfortunately based on real cases.) Paul is discussing trivial matters between Christians within the church. The Corinthians were taking matters to court where they had no jurisdiction, and it was a terrible witness—it still is.

Further examples of such cases include church splits where the members sue each other over who gets to use the name of the old church. That is a horrible witness to the surrounding community. "You want to tell me about reconciliation for eternity, but you can't even agree with your brothers and sisters about a name?" This is among believers! If some neighbor sued the church because its trees had branches hanging over his property, you might understand that. But these are members of the same church, who once were brothers and sisters in Christ— and still supposedly are—but were once brothers and sisters *in the same church*. And now they can't decide who gets to be Third Baptist. It makes no sense. This is Paul's concern: It's a trivial matter that creates a terrible witness.

There is little doubt that these bring the reproach of men upon the church. However, Paul himself resorted to law twice when he was wrongfully arrested as a Roman citizen. He also used the threat of law in Acts 16:37. When one examines the Biblical admonition carefully, there is a clear distinction depending upon the type or nature of the dispute.

> *When one examines the Biblical admonition carefully, there is a clear distinction depending upon the type or nature of the dispute.*

For instance, cases that I handle generally involve serious injuries or death. Any case involving grievous injury or death, by definition, is not at all **"trivial."** I hasten to add that 98% of cases settle without trial, so even the most serious cases rarely see a courtroom. Mediation, which is based on Matthew 18, is often used with great success.

Further, these types of serious disputes are rarely **"between believers"** in any real sense. For instance, if I represent you because you were paralyzed when a truck rear-ended your car, I have to name the negligent driver of the truck (who may be a Christian) in order to obtain the compensation due from his truck insurance. Recall that insurance is purchased to assist in paying for accidental acts that harm another—to help protect one's own assets. It is exceedingly rare for any case to cost an insured driver one penny personally. Many cases are against large corporations that, of course, do not have souls—and therefore cannot be believers. When someone asks me, "Can a Christian sue according to the Bible?" I will ask, "Are you really suing another Christian?"While there are many other types of law, the type that I deal with is mentioned frequently in Scripture: civil injury law. Much of our civil injury law (also called "tort law") is actually based on Biblical passages.

For instance, the law governing dog bites in Tennessee states that if my dog is not known to bite, I likely have no liability for it doing so if it is on my property. However, if my dog has a vicious nature and is known to bite then I can be liable in tort law for all damages. Compare Exodus 21:28–30 (NIV):

> "If a bull gores a man or woman to death, the
> bull is to be stoned to death, and its meat must

not be eaten. But the owner of the bull will not be held responsible. If, however, the bull has had the habit of goring and the owner has been warned but has not kept it penned up and it kills a man or woman, the bull is to be stoned and its owner also is to be put to death. However, if payment is demanded, the owner may redeem his life by the payment of whatever is demanded.[18]

Or look at the law regarding a slip and fall on a premises owned by another. If I create a condition that I know is dangerous and leave it as a virtual trap for another, I am liable in civil damages. Compare Exodus 21:33 (NIV):

If a man uncovers a pit or digs one and fails to cover it and an ox or a donkey falls into it, the owner of the pit must pay for the loss.[19]

Other interesting accidents in Scripture include the negligent attaching of an axe head to an axe handle such that it flies off and kills someone while chopping wood (Deuteronomy 19:5), and the dropping of a stone on an unseen man (Numbers 35:22).

---

[18] Exodus 21:28–30, New International Version.

[19] Exodus 21:33, New International Version.

So someone who maintains that the Bible forbids civil lawsuits is making an interesting argument. They are actually arguing that Moses got it wrong. Moses and the other judges he appointed handled civil law cases according to the rules of Leviticus and Deuteronomy. The whole scenario was designed to handle civil disputes so they did not become criminal disputes: Moses established Cities of Refuge and set repayments amounts. We can all agree a civil lawsuit better handles a dispute than some guy saying, "You injured my son in an accident. Now I'm going to go beat up your son with a baseball bat." Anyone with a third-grade sense of morality knows that is wrong.

Our insurance system is based on the court system, which is based on Leviticus and Deuteronomy. The insurance system exists so we can transfer some of our risk to them (in exchange for payments). If we become liable for a civil offense, the damages will then be paid by the insurance company instead of we ourselves. Of course, our premiums may then skyrocket—a natural consequence and application of personal responsibility.

Our insurance system is based on the court system, which is based on Leviticus and Deuteronomy.

The problem is that insurance companies are in business to deny claims if they can. If they cannot, they attempt to pay as little as possible. Insurance companies are not in business to overpay. As a result, victims of accidents are left without much choice but to go through the system.

That being said, you can act in a way that is permitted but still be a poor witness. The right thing in the wrong way for the wrong reasons, is actually the wrong thing. A greedy or hateful attitude is concerning, and should be a wake-up call to anyone pursuing restitution. Thankfully, out of all the hundreds of injured Christians whom I have represented, the vast majority are the most forgiving and charitable folks you can imagine.

The Bible also says, "And if anyone would sue you and take your tunic, let him have your cloak as well."[20] That guides how Christians who are sued should respond in

---

[20] Matthew 5:40, English Standard Version.

the event you are accused of an offense. Your response should not be pure defiance. Instead, you should respond with generosity and the realization that all things come from the Lord. Take responsibility.

Responsibility goes both ways. If you are the victim of an accident, you are forced to take personal responsibility for your loss. I don't think it's wrong to ask the other side to take responsibility too. And if the offending party is a Christian, he should get on the phone with his insurance company to say, "Pay these people. I caused that accident." When a truck driver walks into mediation and apologizes—"Whatever happens in this case, I'm very sorry that I glanced away and caused this accident. I'm sorry for your loss."—that goes a long way toward resolving the case. It's both biblical and practical.

Responsibility goes both ways.

Lawsuits can force negligent parties to take responsibility for their errors. Sometimes people talk of lawsuits being a way of making another person responsible for one's own misfortune. But if not for lawsuits generally, we might still have Ford Pintos with exploding gas tanks on the road, burning people alive after very minor car accidents. The medicines we take would not be so thoroughly tested. Nursing homes would not be under any incentive to give better care.

To be sure, some cases are biblically forbidden. For instance, a lady offers a prayer request for another lady in a small group. The second woman hears about it, feels it was an invasion of her privacy, and wants to sue for slander. I don't think that would be Biblically valid. No Christian attorney would counsel someone to pursue it. And virtually no aspect of a church split should be handed over to the courts: who receives the building fund, controls the naming rights, keeps the main sanctuary. Those should be handled in accordance with the mediation principles laid down in Matthew chapters 14–18. If someone sins against you, go one-to-one to them first. If that doesn't work bring someone else. Another person may be able to call them out as a brother in Christ, making an impression and pulling them out of the spiral.

Not only can a Christian sue according the Bible— sometimes they should. In many cases I represent children injured in accidents. Their parents are responsible to properly lodge a claim that will be legally approved and secure a recovery. Parents must provide for their children, and accidents can make provision (such as provision of hospital care) exorbitantly costly. Lawsuits can be in accordance with biblical principles.

The Bible says, "But if anyone does not provide for his relatives, and especially for members of his household, he has denied the faith and is worse than an unbeliever."[21] The implication is that you should be prudent about making claims. However, your claim must be proper, with supporting evidence. Allegations are not the same as proof. If your claim relies partly on your own testimony, you must adhere to the highest standards of trustworthiness. In my contract, I stipulate that my clients must not change or color their testimony. Their statements must be reliable. I don't know how many lawyers include that in their contract, but I for one don't want anyone painting matters as better or worse than they are. Deal with things as they are; let your yes be yes and your no be no.

---

[21] 1 Timothy 5:8, English Standard Version.

As you can see, the Bible does not forbid lawsuits, but it gives us much direction. Here is a Biblical checklist that may be helpful in evaluating a potential claim:

1. Is this matter "trivial?" (If so, overlook it.) [1 Corinthians 6:2 and Colossians 3:13]
2. Is this matter solvable by involvement of others at church? [1 Corinthians 6:4 and Matthew 18:15]
3. Are my motives selfish or vengeful? (If so, stop). [Philippians 2:3]
4. Have I tried to resolve my claim before suit or court? [Proverbs 25:8]

In the end, some will say my cases are about money. I understand the criticism. However, as I may tell a jury, "Don't give my client money—give her back *time*...give her back *years of pain*...give her back a life without this *suffering*...give her back her quality of life. But if you cannot give these things, then compensation is all we can ask for. It gives her freedom and it gives her choices. That is all we have to offer her."

"Compensation is all we can ask for. It gives her freedom and it gives her choices. That is all we have to offer her."

Will You Take My Case?

I do not take every case. As I evaluate a potential case, I watch out for the following red flags.

Trust

First and foremost, do I trust the person? Some people give off a bad vibe—you know the type. Thankfully they are few. But if I feel I cannot trust the person, I'm probably not going to take their case, regardless of whatever else happens.

Focusing on Payout

Valuing a case is hard. The rule of thumb used to be that the value of a case is two or three times the cost of the medical bills; however, that rule has gone by the wayside now. Personally, I value cases as much on current evidence and gut feeling as I do on prior results. Because of this complexity, it's usually a bad sign if someone asks me immediately in the very first meeting how much their case is worth. Most of my clients don't.

Contested Liability

Most people think the lawyer's whole purpose in a car accident case is to determine fault. The fact of the matter is that fault is usually the easiest thing to prove. Fault is typically clear, especially in a rear-end accident. The most important issue is not typically how you got hurt—but how hurt you got. That's also what your attorney tries to prove.

> *The most important issue is not typically how you got hurt—but how hurt you got.*

However, there are cases in which liability is almost impossible to figure out. For instance, two people enter the middle lane at exactly the same time from opposing sides. If I cannot determine my client's percentage of fault, the case will benefit neither of us. Fifty percent fault means no driver receives any payout in Tennessee. You might as well be 100% at fault.

It surprises many that the driver who receives the traffic ticket is not thereby proven to be at fault. As a matter of fact, those tickets and accident reports are not even admissible at civil trial. That really surprises people. But because traffic tickets are hearsay—the cop didn't see the accident—they are inadmissible.

It surprises many that the driver who receives the traffic ticket is not thereby proven to be at fault.

Low Property Damage

Another red flag is low property damage. Even though minor damage outside can still have a major impact inside—such as in the 2001 death of NASCAR great Dale Earnhardt—most significant injuries also result in destroyed cars. Even with a less severe injury, pictures of a totaled car help everyone view the injury as reasonable. If you have to get down in the parking lot at a certain angle just to see a scratch on the bumper, it's very difficult to prove there were serious injuries.

Soft Tissue Damage

Soft tissue damage is another red flag. "Soft tissue" is a term of art, but at a basic level it excludes things like fractures and dislocations. It only deals with soreness and pain. This is not a reason to immediately turn the case down—actually, most of these aren't. But in combination, if three or more red flags arise the case gets messy.

Prior Cervical or Back Problems

Prior cervical or back problems tend to be aggravated by any accident. A long history of back and neck problems, possibly with chiropractic treatment, tends to contain many complaints of pain. It's like a chronic diagnosis. That makes it hard to differentiate what happened in this accident unless there are truly new symptoms.

History of Depression or Fibromyalgia

Another issue that must be considered is a long-term history of depression or fibromyalgia. These sorts of chronic problems tend to manifest themselves with mental pain, which is often hard to discern from physical pain. This concern is one I personally evaluate on a case-by-case basis.

Red flags like these may, singly or in combination, cause me to decline a case. Alternatively, I may request more information before committing.

Conclusion.
What Should I Do Now?

I sincerely hope that you have benefited from reading this book. From the frequently asked questions, through the specific types of claims, on to the action steps and more—all equip you to make the right decisions both before and after an accident.

You can visit my blog at PeelLawFirm.com/blog and MemphisChristianInjuryLawyer.com for more legal lessons. I regularly post new material on law-practice-related topics.

On my law practice website, PeelLawFirm.com, you can apply for a free case evaluation. Simply give us enough information to contact you, and you'll hear from us in no time!

I also speak frequently at churches, clubs, and groups at no charge. If you or someone you know is interested in having me speak, contact me using the information below.

The purpose of my practice is to seek justice for those injured by tractor-trailer crashes, car accidents, medical malpractice, and nursing homes. Hopefully I will never have to handle any of these cases for you.

But if you ever need assistance, you know where to find me.

David B. Peel
September 2016

About David

David B. Peel is a lawyer of over 20 years running a small, personal practice. He focuses on serious injury cases, death and disability cases, and tractor-trailer crashes.

David was born in Tennessee, raised in Arkansas, and has lived in Tennessee since he was 21. He worked in a wide variety of jobs during his education, but still excelled in academics.

David is a homeschooling Dad with three teens and a beautiful bride of over 22 years, Trish. He is a fisherman, author, artist, photographer, Bible teacher, missionary, woodworker, natural leader, and family man who loves to travel. He has taken his family on trips to every inhabited continent.

David enjoys a reputation as a successful, caring, Christian lawyer in the area of personal injury law. Passionate about helping his clients through difficult times, David values faith and family above all else. He also writes weekly columns in local papers.

David believes he was called into the law to help people through the hardest challenges of their lives. Serious injury or death of a loved one is something none of us can prepare for. In his practice, David carries the burden of the financial aspects of catastrophic cases so his clients can focus on healing.

David B. Peel
(901) 872-4229
DavidPeel@PeelLawFirm.com
www.PeelLawFirm.com

Peel Law Firm
P.O. Box 8
8582 U.S. Hwy 51 N
Millington, TN 38083-0008

Facebook: https://www.facebook.com/PeelLawFirm
Twitter: https://twitter.com/PeelLawFirm

Copyright

Two Feet or Ten? Perspective Matters: What You Don't See When You Drive

David B. Peel

8582 U.S. Highway 51 North
Millington, TN 38053

Phone: (901) 495-2524
Email: peellawfirm@peellawfirm.com

ISBN-10: 1-946203-07-6
ISBN-13: 978-1-946203-07-6

—Disclaimer—
Although the author and publisher have made every effort to ensure that the information in this book was correct at press time, the author and publisher do not assume and hereby disclaim any liability to any party for any loss, damage, or disruption caused by errors or omissions, whether such errors or omissions result from negligence, accident, or any other cause. The author is only licensed in Tennessee and does not intend to discuss injury cases in other states, as laws there may differ.

www.ExpertPress.net

80848876R00111

Made in the USA
Columbia, SC
23 November 2017